JEWISH AND MANDAEAN INCANTATION BOWLS

in the Royal Ontario Museum

NEAR AND MIDDLE EAST SERIES

1. *The Mosaic Tradition.* By F. V. Winnett
2. *Safaitic Inscriptions from Jordan.* By F. V. Winnett
3. *History and Chronology of the Eighteenth Dynasty of Egypt: Seven Studies.* By Donald B. Redford
4. *Oral Formulaic Language in the Biblical Psalms.* By Robert C. Culley
5. *Jewish and Mandaean Incantation Bowls in the Royal Ontario Museum.* By W. S. McCullough

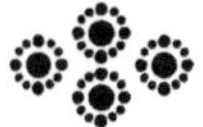

Jewish and Mandaean Incantation Bowls

IN THE ROYAL ONTARIO MUSEUM

W. S. McCullough

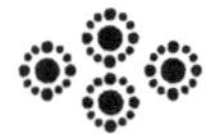

UNIVERSITY OF TORONTO PRESS

Printed in Canada
Reprinted in 2018
ISBN 978-1-4875-7918-0 (paper)

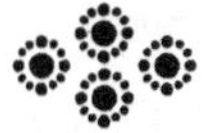

PREFACE

THE FIVE TERRACOTTA BOWLS which are the subject of this study are commonplace in appearance, their only distinction being that each has on its inside surface (and in one case on the outside as well) a spiral inscription in a dialect of Aramaic. The inscriptions are in fact magical texts designed to throw a protective spell over the persons for whom they were written. Bowls of this type have been found in Mesopotamia in considerable numbers during the past century, and have reached the Western world either through dealers or through archaeologists. A collection of thirty-one Mandaean bowls was published by H. Pognon in 1898 (*Inscriptions mandaïtes des coupes de Khouabir*), but the first comprehensive study of such texts was not made until 1913 when J. A. Montgomery presented forty bowls in *Aramaic Incantation Texts from Nippur.* Since then other scholars, notably C. H. Gordon, have enlarged our knowledge of this subject. In the five texts before us we do not therefore claim to present material that is new in principle, for they are akin to the numerous texts already published. Nonetheless, they add in various ways to the lore of the Mesopotamian incantation bowls, and in particular the three Mandaean ones make a modest contribution to the known vocabulary of Mandaic (see the asterisked words in Glossaries 3 and 4). Text D is the most interesting of the ones presented here: although it is in Mandaic, it does not employ the traditional religious terminology of the Mandaeans, and it uses what is almost a novelty in the published magic texts, a number of magic signs to reinforce its verbal incantations.

The author wishes to thank the Royal Ontario Museum, Toronto, for permission to publish these texts, and the staff of the Museum, and especially Miss W. Needler, for supplying all the photographs and for making the bowls available whenever required.

This work has been published with the help of grants from the

Humanities Research Council of Canada, using funds provided by the Canada Council, and from the Publications Fund of the University of Toronto Press.

W. S. M.

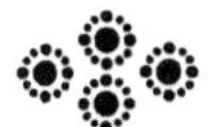

CONTENTS

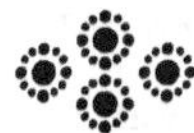

ABBREVIATIONS

AASOR	*Annual of the American Schools of Oriental Research*
AE	C. H. Gordon, "An Aramaic Exorcism," in *AO*, vol. 6 (1934), pp. 466–74
AF	F. Rosenthal, *Die aramäistische Forschung . . .*, 1939
AfO	*Archiv für Orientforschung*
AIB	C. H. Gordon, "Aramaic Incantation Bowls," in *Or*, vol. 10 (1941), pp. 116–41, 272–84, 339–60
AIC	C. H. Gordon, "The Aramaic Incantation in Cuneiform," in *AfO*, vol. 12 (1938), pp. 105–17
AIT	J. A. Montgomery, *Aramaic Incantation Texts from Nippur*, 1913
AJSL	*American Journal of Semitic Languages*
AMB	C. H. Gordon, "Aramaic Magical Bowls . . . Museums," in *AO*, vol. 6 (1934), pp. 319–34
AMMB	C. H. Gordon, "Aramaic and Mandaic Magical Bowls," in *AO*, vol. 9 (1937), pp. 84–106
AO	*Archiv Orientální*
a. part.	active participle
Aph.	Aphel
Aram.	Aramaic
AS	E. A. W. Budge, *Amulets and Superstitions*, 1930
BASOR	*Bulletin of the American Schools of Oriental Research*
B.Heb.	Biblical Hebrew
CPM	E. S. Drower, *The Canonical Prayerbook of the Mandaeans*, 1959
cst.	construct
DESB	R. C. Thompson, *The Devils and Evil Spirits of Babylonia*, vol. 1, 1903; vol. 2, 1904
Ethpa.	Ethpael
Ethpe.	Ethpeel
Etta.	Ettafal
f.	feminine
G	M. Lidzbarski, *Ginza*, 1925
GBA I	J. N. Epstein, "Gloses babylo-araméennes," in *Revue des études juives*, vol. 73 (1921), pp. 27–58
GBA II	J. N. Epstein, *ibid.*, vol. 74 (1922), pp. 40–72
ICGM	H. Pognon, "Une incantation . . . en mandaïte," in *Mémoires de la Société de linguistique de Paris*, vol. 8 (1894), pp. 193–234

IES	C. H. Gordon, "An Incantation in Estrangelo Script," in *Or*, vol. 18 (1949), pp. 336–41
IMCK	H. Pognon, *Inscriptions mandaïtes des coupes de Khouabir*, 1898
imp.	imperfect
imv.	imperative
inf.	infinitive
J	M. Lidzbarski, *Das Johannesbuch der Mandäer*, vol. 2, 1915
JAOS	*Journal of the American Oriental Society*
J.Aram.	Jewish Aramaic
Jast.	M. Jastrow, *A Dictionary of the Targumim* . . . , 1903
JRAS	*Journal of the Royal Asiatic Society*
Justi	F. Justi, *Iranisches Namenbuch*, 1895
l.	line
lit.	literally
ll.	lines
LP	C. H. Gordon, *The Living Past*, 1941
m.	masculine
Mand.	Mandaic
MD	E. S. Drower and R. Macuch, *A Mandaic Dictionary*, 1963
MG	T. Nöldeke, *Mandäische Grammatik*, 1875
MII	E. S. Drower, *The Mandaeans of Iraq and Iran*, 1937
MIT	E. M. Yamauchi, *Mandaean Incantation Texts*, 1966
MP	E. S. Drower, "A Mandaean Phylactery," in *Iraq*, vol. 5 (1938), pp. 31–54
MS	S. A. Pallis, *Mandaean Studies*, 1926
MW	E. S. Drower, "Mandaean Writings," in *Iraq*, vol. 1 (1934), pp. 171–82
MZ	M. Lidzbarski, "Mandäische Zaubertexte," in *Ephemeris . . .Epigraphik*, vol. 1 (1902), pp. 89–106
n.	noun
Or	*Orientalia*
p.	page
Pa.	Pael
Pe.	Peel
per.	person
Pers.	Persian
pf.	perfect
pl.	plural
p.n.	proper noun
pp.	pages
p. part(s).	passive participle(s)
PR	E. S. Drower, "A Phylactery for Rue," in *Or*, vol. 15 (1946), pp. 324–46
prep.	preposition
Q	M. Lidzbarski, *Mandäische Liturgien* ("Qulasta"), 1920
RA	*Revue d'assyriologie*
S	M. Schwab, "Vocabulaire de l'angélologie. . . ," in *Mémoires . . . et belles-lettres*, vol. 10 (1897), pp. 113–430
s.	singular
super.	superscript
Syr.	Syriac
TTQ	E. S. Drower, *The Thousand and Twelve Questions*, 1960

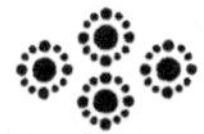

INTRODUCTION

The Date of the Texts

THE DATE OR DATES of our texts cannot be determined except in the most general way. Texts A and B, which are in Jewish Aramaic, appear in script, language, and ideology to be of the same genre as most of Montgomery's Aramaic bowls (AIT). For instance, their use of such verbs as "bind" (B, l. 1), "tie" and "seal" (A, l. 4), "seal" (B, ll. 1, 4), "bind" ("press") (A, l. 2), of words or phrases like "demons" (B, ll. 6, 8), "healing" (B, l. 3), "the signet-ring of El Shaddai" (A, l. 4), "the seal of Shaddai" (B, l. 9), of angelic beings (A, l. 1; B, l. 3), and of nonsense syllables (B, ll. 5–9) all have parallels in AIT. The scripts of Texts A and B are similarly very close to some of the scripts exhibited in Montgomery's bowls. While such similarities furnish no conclusive proof about the date, they give some support to the view that these texts could have been produced about the same time and in the same general environment as those of Montgomery's bowls. The latter are given a *terminus ad quem* of about 600 A.D.,[1] largely on the basis of Peters' account of the excavation in which they were found in 1888–89. If we accept this evidence, Texts A and B may therefore date roughly in the period which produced the Babylonian Talmud.

In dating Texts C, D, and E, which are in Mandaic, we have to keep in mind three considerations. First, as a *terminus a quo* there would be the emergence of the Mandaeans as a distinct religious community and the development of Mandaic as a dialect of Aramaic. It is improbable that either of these could have occurred before the first century A.D. Second, as a *terminus ad quem* we must recall that Montgomery's study (AIT) includes three Mandaean texts which were part of Peters' Nippur find and for which 600 A.D. seems to be a terminal date. If Texts C, D, and E could

[1]AIT, pp. 102–5.

be shown to be more closely related to the Mandaean bowls in AIT than to the other published Mandaean texts, this might favour 600 A.D. as a *terminus ad quem* for them. It is impossible, however, to establish this closer relationship, for our present texts have as many connections with other Mandaean bowls as with those in AIT. We can only note that Text C is said to have come from Nippur, and in this case Montgomery's suggested terminal date may be relevant to it. Third, it can be urged, since there is no evidence—either linguistic or conceptual—of Arabic or Muslim influence in our texts, that they date from pre-Islamic times. Against this, we must remember that magic practices have a very old history among the Mandaeans, and also that the use of incantation bowls still persists among them.[2] Such incantations do not necessarily bear any evidence of the age in which they were written. Further, these texts are commonly produced by priests,[3] who are unlikely to utilize much material that is obviously non-Mandaean. In conclusion, we cannot be at all sure of the dates of Texts C, D, and E, although probably they are pre-Islamic.

The Praxis and History of the Magic Bowl

The magical procedure associated with incantation bowls can only be surmised. That the magic bowl is a kind of talisman or phylactery, intended to cope with certain evil beings or circumstances, is obvious. But why the spell itself should have been written on a bowl, and upon the inside of a bowl, is not clear. Nor can we account fully for the peculiar position in which such bowls have usually been found. Montgomery's bowls, for instance, which were discovered in the earth either under the ruins of houses or in a cemetery, were mostly in an upside-down position, i.e., with the open mouth downward.[4] Pognon gives the same report about the position of his bowls.[5] Several of Pognon's specimens may have been intended for use in cemeteries for they are inscribed D̠ BYT QWBRY'.[6] On the basis of this evidence we may assume that the bowls were commonly deposited either under the floors of houses or in cemeteries, and that they served as phylacteries. On the proceedings connected with the actual burial of a bowl we have no information. E. M. Yamauchi has recently suggested that "the incantation would be recited in a voice that was not a normal one."[7]

[2]MII, pp. 25, 348.

[3]MII, pp. xviii, xxiii.

[4]AIT, pp. 13–14, 41. For a photograph of some bowls in this position *in situ*, see H. V. Hilprecht, *The Excavations in Assyria and Babylonia* (Philadelphia, 1904), p. 448.

[5]IMCK, p. 3.

[6]E.g., bowl 5 in IMCK.

[7]"Aramaic Magic Bowls," in *JAOS*, vol. 85 (1965), p. 522.

While there is no completely satisfactory theory to explain the upside-down position of the magic bowls, H. Hyvernat first proposed that the bowls were really prison-houses for the demons, the latter being kept in confinement by the surrounding incantation.[8] Pognon held a similar view,[9] and this explanation was endorsed by Montgomery.[10] C. H. Gordon doubted whether people would want demons, even when locked up, on their premises, and he suggested that the inverted bowl is reminiscent of mortuary magic, and especially of some magical practice connected with the human skull.[11] This suggestion may be pertinent to those relatively few cases in which two bowls have been found together, open face to open face, but for most of the bowls Hyvernat's proposal seems the more attractive.

None of the editors of the published bowls has commented upon the fact that the incantation is normally inscribed on the inside surface of the bowl, which is obviously the more difficult side to write on. Even in the small number of instances in which the text is found on both sides, it always begins on the interior: apparently the outside is used only in lieu of further space on the inside. This supports the view that there is some special significance to the inside of the bowl and seems to argue against Gordon's attempt to link the bowls with skulls. The three skulls referred to by Montgomery have their inscriptions on their exteriors,[12] and there is no evidence that magical plaques were ever inserted within such skulls. There must, then, have been some cogent reason or some ancient tradition for choosing the semispherical bowl for the incantation, for if an ordinary charm were desired, there would have been no need to use the awkward writing surface afforded by a bowl. Again, if the bowl were merely an example of the use of the magic circle in a spell,[13] a round, flat object would have served the purpose equally well. We therefore return to Hyvernat's view, though we might modify it slightly and give the incantation bowl a twofold function, first to ward off evil after the manner of a common household talisman and, second, to imprison in a kind of devil-trap such demons as do not have enough sense to stay away. The buried, inverted bowl may have enjoyed some additional prestige because the spell was written on its interior: its text thereby had a certain protection against damage from the outside, as the survival of the bowls through the centuries attests.

Since the incantation bowls so far published all come from the Tigris-Euphrates area and all belong to the Christian era and the majority to the first six centuries, it may be inferred that the inscribed bowl was an

[8] *Zeitschrift für Keilschriftforschung*, vol. 2 (1885), pp. 136–9.
[9] IMCK, p. 3.
[10] AIT, pp. 41–42.
[11] LP, p. 199.
[12] AIT, p. 256.
[13] See index of AS, under "circle" and "disk."

innovation in magical technique which came into vogue only in the early Christian centuries. We would nevertheless suppose, despite the novelty of the practice, that the basic antecedents of the magic bowl would be found in Mesopotamia. Magic, in its various ramifications, flourished in this region as far back as Sumerian times, but specific sources of the later incantation bowl are difficult to discover. We can disregard the notion, so common in the bowls, that a spell "binds" a supernatural being, for this is a first premise of magic the world over. Montgomery, who summed up his research into this matter in AIT, pointed out, as one source of bowl magic, the Assyrian custom of burying figurines (of humans, animals, gods) under the threshold or floors of houses to protect the dwellers from evil spirits.[14] The *âšipu* priest would undoubtedly accompany the burial with a proper incantation. Montgomery might have noted that in one incantation tablet the following is found: "I deposited bitumen underneath the . . . of the door that Ea may rest within the house."[15] This seems to suggest that the divine power could be kept in a given spot by physical means. Montgomery also cited a Babylonian spell intended to lay low a house demon. The passage in question is from the "Tablet of the Ban," and the relevant words are:

May the fish-trap (*gišparru*) of Ea catch him [i.e., the demon],
May the net (*sapâru*) of Nisaba entrap him . . .
May a bowl which ought not to be opened (*kakkulti la patê*) cover him.[16]

We do not know what actions were associated with this incantation: possibly a fish-net or a mixing-bowl was used in the manner of sympathetic magic to supplement the spoken words. But this second quotation is the only one of its sort in the two volumes of DESB, and it scarcely justifies Montgomery's assertion that "the praxis of bowl magic existed in ancient Babylonia,"[17] an assertion repeated later, but with as little proof, by Gordon.[18] Various divining vessels were of course familiar in ancient Mesopotamia, but the connection between them and our inscribed bowls is by no means obvious.

In December 1963, C. H. Gordon offered a paper before the Archaeological Institute of America in which he noted the discovery at Knossus, Crete, of bowls in an upside-down position with spells written spirally on their interiors.[19] If this interpretation of the archaeological data can be sustained, it would point to the incantation bowl as being a fairly old form of magic. This being so, it is strange that after its Minoan appearance the magic bowl seems to have fallen into disuse, to reappear

[14]AIT, pp. 42–44.
[15]DESB, vol. 1, p. 111, ll. 305–6, revised by R. F. G. Sweet.
[16]DESB, vol. 2, pp. 120–5, revised by R. F. G. Sweet.
[17]AIT, p. 43.
[18]AMMB, p. 84.
[19]*American Journal of Archaeology*, vol. LXVIII (1964), pp. 194–5.

in western Asia only in the early Christian centuries. What influences brought about its revival in the latter period we do not know, but its use by Christians, Jews, and Mandaeans indicates that its popularity was quite extensive.

The Mandaeans

As the most important texts in the present study are in Mandaic, a brief sketch of the Mandaeans is offered here as a complement to the later notes.

The Mandaeans of today are a minority group living in parts of Iraq and Iran and known popularly as the Subba. Most of them are in southern Iraq; the Iraq census of 1962 put their number at 11,825. While they ordinarily speak Iraqi Arabic, the language of their religion is Mandaic, a dialect of Aramaic, though this is understood only by their priests.

The religious literature of the Mandaeans, all of it in Mandaic, may here be noted. Their chief book is the Ginza or Great Treasure, also called the Great Book. This is a heterogeneous collection of prayers, hymns, and treatises of a theological, mythological, and historical character. Most of it seems to have been put into its present form in the Sasanian period (224–651 A.D.). Another work of importance is the Teaching of the Kings, commonly known as the Book of John. Its contents are almost as variegated as those of the Ginza. It takes its common designation from the fact that about one-fifth of it is devoted to an account of John the Baptist, amplifying the four references to John found in the Ginza. A third document, the Book of Souls, also known as the Qulasta, contains the liturgies used on various occasions. This was edited and translated by M. Lidzbarski in 1920 (*Mandäische Liturgien*). A fuller edition of this is now available in E. S. Drower's work, *The Canonical Prayerbook of the Mandaeans* (1959).

The history of the Mandaeans is very imperfectly known. Direct European evidence of their presence in Mesopotamia takes us back only to the sixteenth century. It is probable, however, that the Mandaean insistence upon flowing ("living") water for their religious lustrations has operated for hundreds of years to keep them near the great rivers of Iraq. Moreover, the internal evidence of the Ginza suggests that at one time the Mandaeans lived under Sasanian (and possibly Parthian) kings, which would seem to confirm the view that the Mandaean community has been somewhere near its present habitat since before the Muslim era began. This conclusion is strengthened by the references to the Sabaeans in the Quran.[20] On various grounds these Quranic Sabaeans,

[20] 2:59; 5:73; 22:17.

who constituted one of the three non-Muslim sects of early Islam, are identified with the Mandaeans. If this identification is justified, it implies that the Mandaeans were a sizable group in the non-Arab regions in the pre-Islamic period. This supposition is confirmed when we consider the peculiar dialect of Aramaic used by the Mandaeans. It is highly improbable that this could have been acquired or developed after the conquests of Islam, when Arabic came into general use in the Semitic-speaking areas of the Near East. Actually the Aramaic script used by the Mandaeans, whose earliest form is displayed in the incantation bowls, seems to be a development of that used in the Nabataean and Palmyrene inscriptions.

The early history of the Mandaeans, as well as their origin, is a highly speculative matter and need not detain us. The place given by them to John the Baptist and their use of the word "jordan" to designate any source of flowing water seem to point to some remote connection with Palestine or with either the Christian or Jewish traditions.

What has kept the Mandaean community a compact body all through the centuries has been its distinctive religious faith, the core of which is best described as a primitive fertility cult. This view is supported by the references in the Ginza to the Great Fruit as some primal entity,[21] and to Life or the Great Life (see notes on "Life" in Text C, ll. 1, 16). Further confirmation of this opinion comes from the fact that no historical founder of their religion appears in the Mandaean tradition. How early the idea of Light, with the concomitant concept of an opposing Darkness, became associated with Fruit and Life is uncertain. But whatever this faith may have started with, it is evident that during the pre-Islamic era it came under the influence of the various cults flourishing at that time in western Asia—Christianity, Gnosticism, Judaism, Manichaeism, Mithraism, and Zoroastrianism. The result was that the earlier ideas of the Mandaeans were considerably modified and supplemented, not always in an orderly and consistent fashion. The Ginza may be taken as a reflection of the theological confusion of this period. Throughout these changes, the central rite of the Mandaeans, baptism in flowing water (the latter a symbol of Life and Light), remained unchanged.

The Mandaean priests, who serve at baptisms, births, deaths, marriages, etc., also function as the community's astrologers. For the Mandaeans believe that the stars and the planets are under the control of the King of the Light, and that the lives of men are in some way influenced by the heavenly bodies. Therefore before performing any important act or reaching any important decision, the faithful consult the priests to learn if the heavens are giving their benediction. Along with their astrological expertise, the priests are also adept at the writing of charms and amulets. For while magic is frowned upon in the Ginza,[22] it is too well established

[21] G, p. 65, l. 32.

[22] G, p. 16, l. 28; p. 80, l. 29.

a means of combating life's dangers and ills to be lightly brushed aside. It is therefore probable that two of the Mandaean texts (C and E) in this study were written by priests; there is some doubt about this in the case of Text D.

While the Mandaean texts in this present study shed some further light on magic as practised among the Mandaeans, they are of special interest for the small additions they make to Mandaic lexicography. Words that are asterisked in Glossaries 3 and 4 are words, or forms of words, that do not appear in Drower and Macuch, *A Mandaic Dictionary*.

JEWISH AND MANDAEAN INCANTATION BOWLS

in the Royal Ontario Museum

NOTE ON THE FOLLOWING TEXTS

In the texts, following the practice of the bowl-writers, the same letter, in this case *Heth*, will be used for both *He* and *Heth*.

Dots under Hebrew letters indicate doubtful readings.

Dots on the line indicate illegible or missing letters or words.

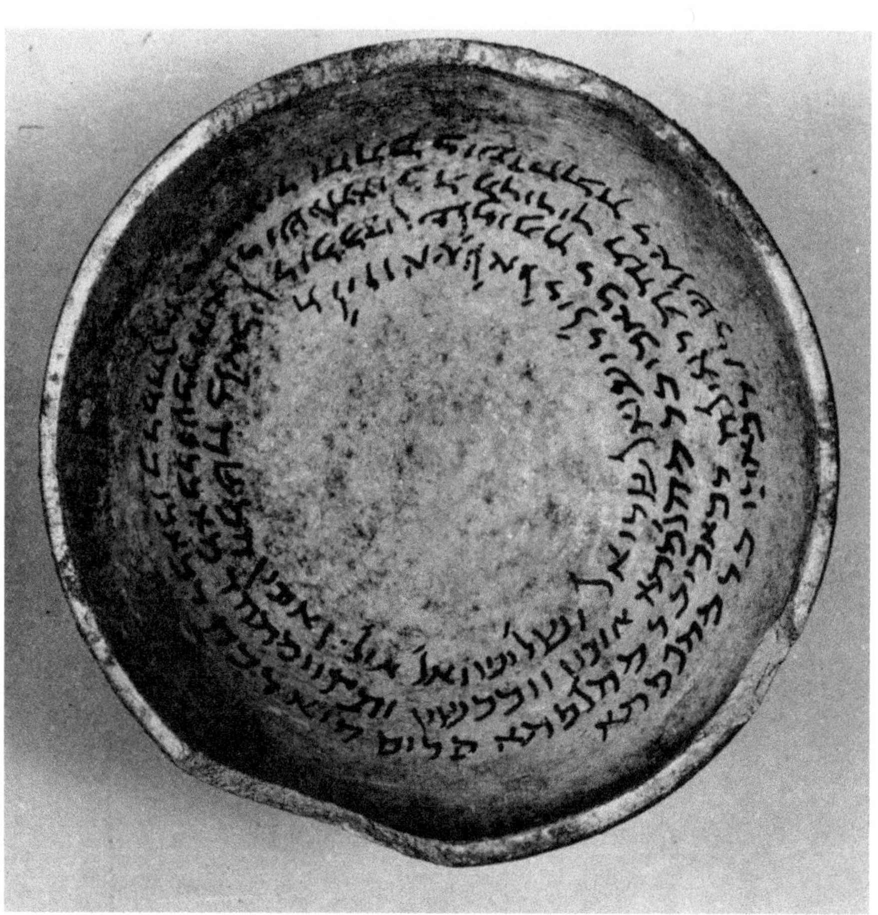

BOWL A (907.1.1)

Introduction

THIS SMALL BOWL (height, 4.8 cm.; diameter at top, 11.7 cm.; thickness, 0.3 cm.) has a short spiral inscription in Jewish Aramaic on its interior. This wording serves as a protective spell for the household of Babai, son of Maḥlapta. It may be presumed that both the bowl-writer and his client were Jewish.

Text

(1) חליזיא אילאיל דילריעיאל שריאל ושלישיאל
אזלון אתון חמשה מלאכין (2) די ממרין על
ביתה ד̱ באבי בר מחלפתא אובין ויכבשון ית
קיימתחד מאברזין ברחיא (3) ירושילְמאי בת
מרודוך תחת ריגילה ד̱ באבי בר מחלפתא קריסתיא
רבת ד̱ באבי בר מחלפתא (4) ד̱ ציר וחתם
ביעזקתה ד̱ אל שדי ד̱ באבי בר מחלפתא̇

Translation

(1) Girt are El-El, Dilri'iel, Sariel, and Shlishiel; be gone, ye five angels (2) who are afflicting the house of Babai, son of Maḥlapta, with ghosts; and they will bind Qyymthd M'brzyn with a millstone; (3) the Jerusalemite, daughter of Mruduk, (is) under the protection (or "good luck")

of Babai, son of Maḫlapta, (and of) Qristia, mistress of Babai, son of Maḫlapta; (4) this (lit. "which") is tied and sealed with the signet-ring of El Shaddai belonging to Babai, son of Maḫlapta.

Commentary

1. *Girt*: in J. Aram. ḤLZ is normally used in the Pa., but the related root ḤLṢ appears in the Pe. in J.Aram., Mand., and Syr. As used in the present text, the word suggests that the four enumerated angels are available to protect the house of Babai.

El-El (ʾYLʾYL): in AIT, bowl 13, l. 7, this appears as a divine name, and in Mandaean literature ʿYL ʿYL serves as a term for the sun-god (G, p. 25, l. 8; p. 43, l. 2); here it is the name of an angel (so also in S, p. 167).

Dilriʿiel (DYLRYʿYʾL) is not found elsewhere; it may have some connection with "friend of El."

Sariel (ŠRYʾL), "my prince is El," appears as a good angel in AIT, IMCK, and S (cf. ŠARYʿYL in MD, p. 446).

Shlishiel (ŠLYŠYʾL): this name, basically B.Heb. ("officer of El"), appears in S, p. 367.

Be gone (ʾZLWN): the imv. ending in N is uncommon in J. Aram. of the Talmud, but it is found in Palestinian Aram., Mand., and Syr.

Five angels: "angel" is here used of a malevolent being; fallen angels are known in Jewish circles as early as the Book of Enoch (64–69). The reference in our text is presumably to the beings who control the five planets; see the note on this phrase in Text C, l. 6.

2. *Who are afflicting* (MMRYN): this is taken to be the a. part. Aph. of MRR.

Babai (BʾBY) appears as a personal name in AIT (p. 275); cf. the B.Heb. name Bebai (Ezr. 8:11) and the Jewish name Baba found in Jast. (p. 136). Justi (p. 54) records both Baba and Babhai.

Maḫlapta (MHLPTʾ) appears as a female name in both J.Aram. and Mand. (see AIT, p. 278); cf. the Mandaean angel MHALPIʿIL in MD, p. 259. Originally this name may have meant that its bearer served as a replacement for a lost child (cf. HLP, Pa. and Aph., "exchange," etc.).

Ghosts: some of the earlier Jewish texts display an interest in ghosts (AIT, p. 82; bowl 20, p. 201; bowl 25, p. 207), but the present text appears to be the only incantation in which the B.Heb. ʾWB appears.

DMW'T' ("effigies") is found in Mand. in Text C, l. 17, and in AIT, bowl 39, l. 9 (cf. DMW DMW, in Text E, l. 16).

They will bind: the subject is either impersonal or it is the four angels named in l. 1. The verb is followed by YT indicating the direct object.

QYYMTHD M'BRZYN: this may be nonsense and be intended to betoken unspecified demons. The only sense that I can extract from it is to suppose that THD is an error for THT, which permits the rendition "the One who is present beneath the stingers," the last word denoting demons, and being the a. part. Aph. of BRZ, "bore."

3. *YRWŠYLM'Y*: this must be "Jerusalemite," but the orthography is peculiar; the ending 'Y is reminiscent of the ending of some Mandaean names (see "Bzurgantai" in Text C, l. 3). This person is evidently a member of Babai's household, but her status is not clear.

Mruduk (MRWDWK): this is the most probable reading of the text but the usual difficulty exists of distinguishing between D and R. This name, which appears nowhere else, may be a variant of MYRDWK, which is found as a woman's name in two of Montgomery's bowls (AIT, bowl 7, l. 10; bowl 27, l. 8). Montgomery suggested a derivation of this name from the Pers. *Mer-ducht*[1] (cf. the note on "Duktan" in Text C, l. 2). A less likely source is B.Heb. MRDK, "Marduk."

Under the protection (lit. "under the foot"): for this same phrase, but in a different sense, see a Mand. text in AIT (bowl 38, ll. 12–13). The vocalization of "foot" (RYGYL) is anomalous.

Qristia (QRYSTY') appears nowhere else. It is improbable that it is a shortened or misspelled form of "Christian" (cf. Syr. KRYṢṬYN'; Mand. K'R'ṢṬY'NY' (pl.) with the variant K'R'SṬY'NY'). More probably it comes from QRS (in Syr. "become dried up," "be rugged"); hence perhaps here "the wizened one" or "the rugged one."

Mistress (RBT): the usual term in other Jewish texts for "wife" is 'NTT' (with various spellings).

4. *Tied and sealed*: these verbs appear in combination in other texts (e.g., AIT, bowl 6, l. 6; bowl 7, l. 2). The present text HTM is presumed to be intended for HTYM.

Signet-ring: BY'ZQTH must be an error for B'YZQTH.

The signet-ring of El Shaddai: this phrase occurs in AIT, bowl 8, l. 11 and bowl 17, l. 12. Not enough is known about the praxis of bowl-magic to judge whether the bowl was in some way physically sealed, or whether the sealing was purely figurative.

[1]Justi, pp. 207–8, under "Mithra."

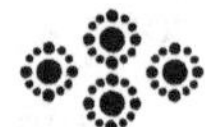

BOWL B (907.1.2)

Introduction

THIS BOWL (height 5.2 cm.; diameter at top, including the brim, 14 cm.; thickness, 0.3 cm.) presents the novelty of a flat brim, 1.5 cm. wide. The inscription in Jewish Aramaic on the interior is for the benefit of one Jannai bar Zkut. A minor reason for including this text in the present study is that it illustrates how badly written and how badly preserved an inscription such as this can be. In many places the writing is entirely or almost entirely illegible.

Text

(1) ..ח כל חטרין אסירין חתימין ... ...
(2) פגרו על ייניי בר זכות ... רוח ... ...
..יא גיוריו (3) בישח וחיילי אסותא ייפצו
ביתא ודירא ... ... ד ברזחות רזחאל יי
(4) חותתא יעדיך זגוס ביש ד בבר ייניי בר
זכות ... .ן ובסירין חתימין וכתייתין
(5) כתב ייניי זבביתיל ח.. קזייז ייחזחזיא
איזון ... ... חשיזז ... ית חימידא
(6) חוס בייניי זכדש ד יי ורוח.. ... ודיויי

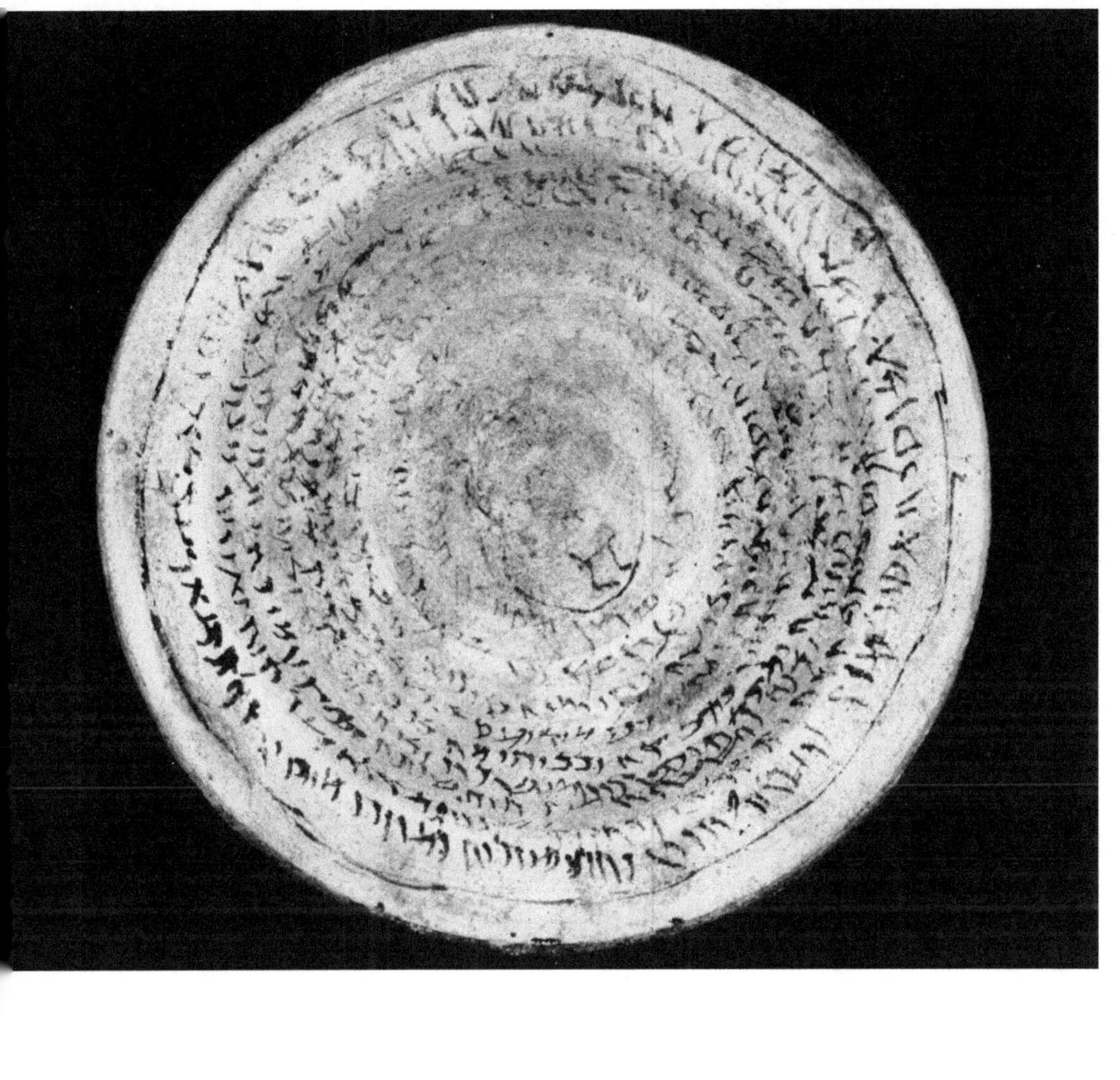

ברא תרחיב ... ... ריות בויזצח ד ולי חל..יי
ד יורוווו ולנח (7) לחש.עווור ..ווריח שותח
תתקון לידח יורוור מן ... ... איין
... חוס ביאף ת.ח.. (8) ... ...
אמחי ערחוחזא וווור ייביי שאורי דיויא סאנסות
ויור כנח ווור אחין אלן סנייא סימאן
ז.וור (9) כול ווורן זוורזווורזווח
ואוורואייין דחיתמא ד שדא וסימאן דורוחות
שמר.דוי גדיא ייייו

Translation

(1) . . . . fenced in (or "whipped"), bound, sealed . . . . (2) they worked destruction against Jannai bar Zkut . . . . GYWYWYW (3) evil (or "his evil") and the powers of healing will deliver the house and the shed . . . . of bar Zkut. Razhcl YY (4) HWTT' will clear out the evil Zgus which is in bar Jannai bar Zkut . . . . and despised, sealed, and crushed. (5) Jannai wrote ZBBYTYL . . . . he cut off YYYHZHZY' . . . . desirable (6) protect Jannai Zkush whom YY and RWH . . . . and the demons of the outdoors it (or "you") shall frighten away . . . . of WWWWWWWW and . . . . . . (7) he uttered a charm 'WWWW . . . . you (pl.) shall pull out LYDH YWWWWW from . . . . verily . . . . protect . . . . (8) . . . . I will smite 'RHWHZ' WWWWW. Jannai placed ("constrained"?) the demons S'NSWT and YWWKNHWWWW 'HYN 'LN (or "gods," or "our god") 'LN, the hateful ones; the formula W.WWW (9) all WWWWN ZWWW ZWWWWZWWH and 'WWWW'YYYYN of the seal of Shaddai and the formula of . . . . the genii YYYYW

Commentary

At the bottom of the interior of the bowl there is a rough circle, inside of which at one time there was evidently a crude figure, doubtless representing some malevolent being, but only the two feet of which are now visible. On the use of the circle in the magic bowls, see the first note on Text C. For illustrations of figures within circles, see AIT, plates II, IV, XIII, XIX; AIB, plates 1, 3 (pp. 132, 134).

1. *HṬRYN*: this seems to be the text, which may be intended for the p. part. Pe.

Fenced in, bound, sealed: Montgomery has drawn attention to the frequent use of such verbs as these in the magic bowls (AIT, pp. 52–53), for the aim of most incantations is to restrict and if possible nullify demonic activity (cf. Text C, ll. 3–8; Text E, ll. 15–17).

2. *PGRW*: 3rd per. pl. pf. Pa.

YYNYY: this is presumably the Jewish name Jannai, usually written YN'Y or YNYY.

ZKWT: this spelling occurs also in l. 4; in l. 3 we have ZHWT, although the text could be read as ZHWS; in l. 6 an uncertain text seems to be ZKWŠ. I can find no other example of ZKWT ("merit," "benefit") being used as a human name, though I note that Schwab records it as the name of an angel (S, p. 234).

RWH: this can be "spirit," but the later occurrences of these same letters (ll. 6, 9) shed no light on their meaning in their present context.

GYWYWYW: this is the first instance in this text of a nonsense word made up of a meaningless group of letters of the alphabet. While other clear examples occur in ll. 6, 7, 8, and 9, it is probable that some of the words in the text which cannot be identified grammatically are also nonsense and thought to have magical potency. Another example of this nonsense is in Text D (ll. 15, 17), where letters of the alphabet, either singly or in groups, appear in conjunction with a number of magic signs. On this use of letters and syllables as charms, see AIT, pp. 59–61.

3. *YYPṢW*: 3rd per. pl. imp. Aph. of PṢY, "deliver."

DYR': if this is the correct reading, we have "cattle-(or "wood-")shed"; if we read DWR', the meaning is "dwelling-place" (AIT, bowl 32, l. 11; cf. MD, p. 105).

Razhel (RZH'L): this is probably the name of an angel, although RZḤ is an unlikely Aram. root. We may have a variant of the Jewish angel Raziel, RZY'L (Jast., p. 1465); Schwab records both RZY'L and RH'L (S, p. 358). Alternatively, this may be an error for RHZYL found in Mand. (IMCK, p. 97; MD, p. 419).

YY (also in l. 6): if this is a separate word, which is uncertain, it must be the familiar abbreviation of Adonai, the Jewish LORD.

4. *Y'DYR*: the verb is presumably ʿDR I, "hoe." If the first Y is part of the word, it is the imp. Pa.; if this Y belongs to the previous word, we have the p. part. Pe.

Zgus (ZGWS): the text is quite legible, but the G seems oddly written. Another less probable reading is Z'S. We may, in either case, have a garbled form of Zeus, for which the Syr. is ZWS, and the J.Aram. ZʿWZ' (AIT, bowl 19, l. 17).

5. *He cut off* (QZYYZ) is probably the Pa. of QZZ, a variant of the more familiar QṢṢ (Jast., p. 1345).

6. *Protect* (HWS) is the imv. of ḤWS; this seems to appear also in l. 7.

RWH: if this is a complement to YY, Jewish usage would lead us to expect RWH QWDŠ', "the Holy Spirit."

Demons (DYWYY): this word (s. DYW'), fairly common in Syr. and Mand., is almost unknown in Jewish literature.[1] It is, however, found in some of the Aramaic incantations, most of which appear to be Jewish (AIT, bowl 2, l. 6; bowl 5, l. 2; etc).

TRHYB is apparently the Aph. of RHB with the meaning "make to hasten." This meaning is supported by Mand. and Syr., but it is not recorded by Jastrow (Jast., p. 1453).

7. *LHŠ*: the L is unusually written, resembling an enlarged Z. The form seems to be the pf. Pe.

TTQWN is the 2nd per. m. pl. imp. Pe. of NTQ.

LYDH: cf. the J.Aram. LYDH, "birth."

'YYN may be the particle 'YN, "verily," "truly," of which 'YYYYN in l. 9 may be another variation.

8. *Š'WY* is the Pa. of *ŠWY*.

Š'NSWT: the reading is most uncertain: the ending WT looks like a Hebraism for the f. pl. It would be suitable to the context to have some form of S'YN', "hateful" or "filthy" (see note on "hateful" in Text C. l. 17), but the support for such a reading is tenuous (cf. SNYY' later in this line).

'HYN: cf. 'HN, an angel mentioned by Schwab (S, p. 162).

'LN (twice) is possibly the demonstrative "these" (usually written 'YLYN). It could also be from 'L, "god," and represent "our god" or "gods."

SNYY': I assume that this is an error for SYNY', which is defective for S'YNY'.

[1] See J. Levy and H. L. Fleischer, *Wörterbuch über die Talmudim*, vol. 1 (Leipzig, 1876), p. 393.

Formula (SYM'N) appears also in l. 9. Literally "sign," the meaning here is probably "magic formula."

9. *HYTM'* (the Y is superscript): this spelling is found in AIT (p. 289), but the commoner J.Aram. is a f. noun ḤTYMT'.

ŠD': the same orthography for Shaddai is recorded in AIT, p. 273.

The last five or six words in this line are very uncertain. We may in WRWH have a word which Schwab cites as one of the names of Metatron (S, p. 231); on Metatron, see the note in Text D, l. 6. The third last word ŠMR.WY must be related in some way to the root ŠMR, "watch," "guard."

GDY' is the pl. of GD', "luck," "genius."

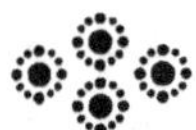

BOWL C (931.4.1)

Introduction

THIS BOWL was purchased in Baghdad in 1931 by Professor T. J. Meek of the University of Toronto, its provenance being given as Nippur. It is a poorly made bowl of rather heavy ware (height 7.2 cm.; diameter at top, 19.9 cm.; diameter at base, 8.4 cm.; thickness, 0.7 cm.), which has a break on one side at the top, thereby creating gaps in five of the twenty-six lines making up the Mandaic inscription. The latter is written on the inside and outside of the bowl, and is the work of at least two hands. The writing, especially on the interior, is rather awkward and careless, but this may be due in part to the grit holes which mar the bowl's surface.

The inscription itself seems to be in three parts. (i) The first, ll. 1–15, is an incantation written for a woman, Duktan Pruk, daughter of Bzurgantai. It was begun on a fresh bowl and covers the whole of the interior and about a line and a half of the exterior. Owing to the break in the bowl, ll. 10–12 and 14–15 are incomplete and are therefore not fully intelligible. There is some evidence of erasures in this part of the incantation, but as far as I can judge, the erasing was done by the original writer. There are also about a dozen words, or parts of words, written between the lines, but as nearly all of these dovetail into the adjacent text, we may assume that they are corrections by the same writer. The spell was evidently intended to protect only the person of Duktan Pruk. There are no references in these lines to her home, her husband, or her family.

(ii) The second part commences with "let the healing" in l. 15, and is by a different hand from that of the first. This part of the charm appears to end when we come to the Mandaean doxology "And Life is victorious!" in l. 16. A line drawn around the bowl at this point separates what follows from what precedes. The apparent purpose of this addition to the original incantation is to throw a protective screen over the woman's dwelling, her spouse, sons, and daughters. The last element in her name is here spelled BZRGWNT'Y.

(iii) The third part, which on epigraphic grounds could be from the same writer as ll. 15–16, covers the rest of the exterior of the bowl, ll. 16–25, and probably also the bottom, l. 26. Its chief purpose is to safeguard the foetus in Duktan Pruk's womb, though the woman's family is mentioned once at the very end. Probably a pregnancy called forth this part of the inscription. In these lines the last element in the client's name is BZWRGWNT'Y (ll. 17, 19) and BZWRGWN'T'Y (l. 22). These differences in the spelling of Bzurgantai lend support to the view that the latter part of the inscription was written by a different hand (or hands) from that responsible for ll. 1–15.

The tripartite character of the incantation seems to reflect two and possibly three stages in Duktan Pruk's life. The first of these might be her premarital days, and the second and third two different times in her marital period. Our bowl would thus have a somewhat unusual history, for, if it was buried somewhere after the original inscription was put on it, it would have had to be unearthed for the writing of the additional lines and then reburied.

While our incantation displays certain internal phenomena which suggest that it is not a unity, it none the less assumes in all its parts a common background of Mandaean belief. For instance, all the angelic and demonic beings mentioned in the text, with the possible exception of Hurmiṣ in l. 6, are known to us from other Mandaean sources. We may conclude that this bowl was inscribed by a Mandaean or Mandaeans, and that it was intended for a Mandaean client.

Text

/ / indicates the break in the bowl.
( ) indicates interlinear writing.

(1) בשומאיחון ד̲ חייא ..א (2) ע̣ס̣ותא תיחוילא
דוכתן פרוך פת (3) בזורגאנתאי עסיריאא באתיא
ד̲ עשיול בראזא עזלעורי (4) תיחין עסיריא גירמיא
מיתיא עסיריא חרביא סייפיא (5) פ̣א̣י̣ג̣ מומיא ד̲
בי דבאביא עסירא זיקא ד̲ באיתא ד̲ פתחיל פכיר
(6) חאמשא מלאכיא ד̲ אלמא חאזין עסיר חורמיץ
סחרא תותיא (7) מיא תיתאייא ועלאייא מיא עסיר

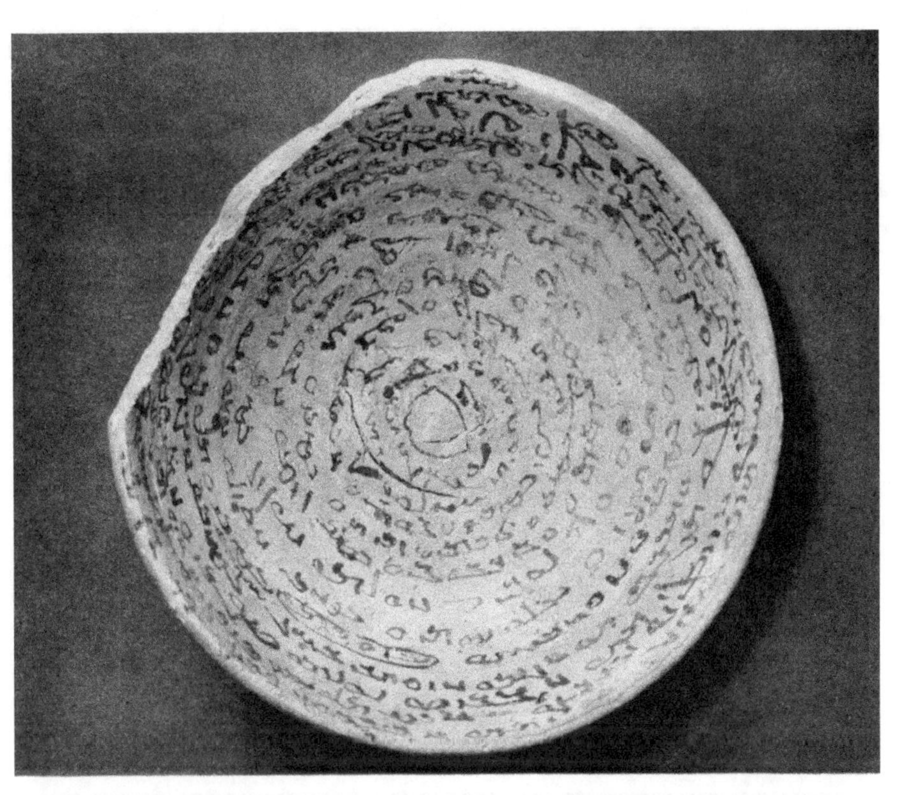

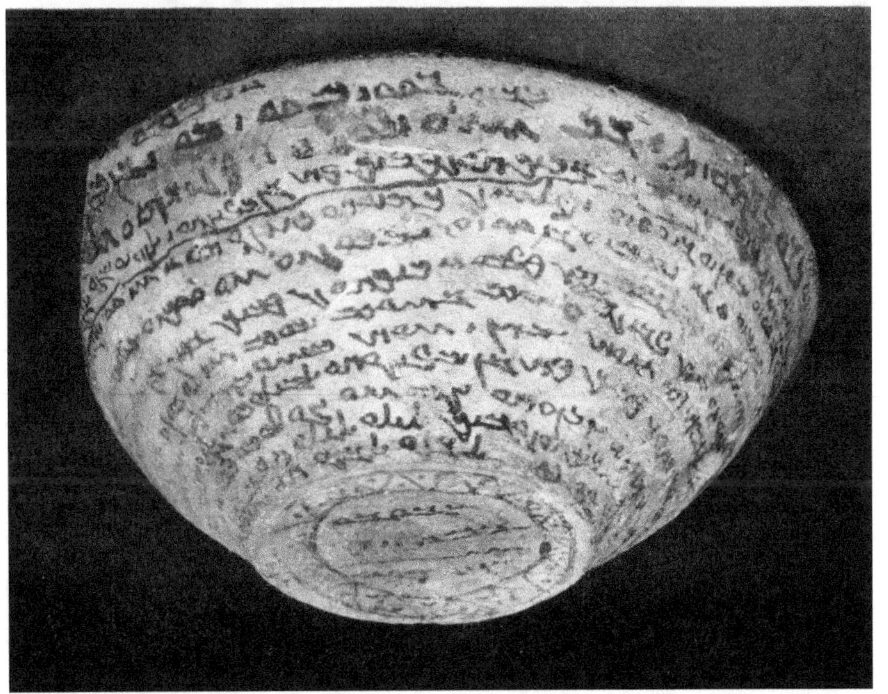

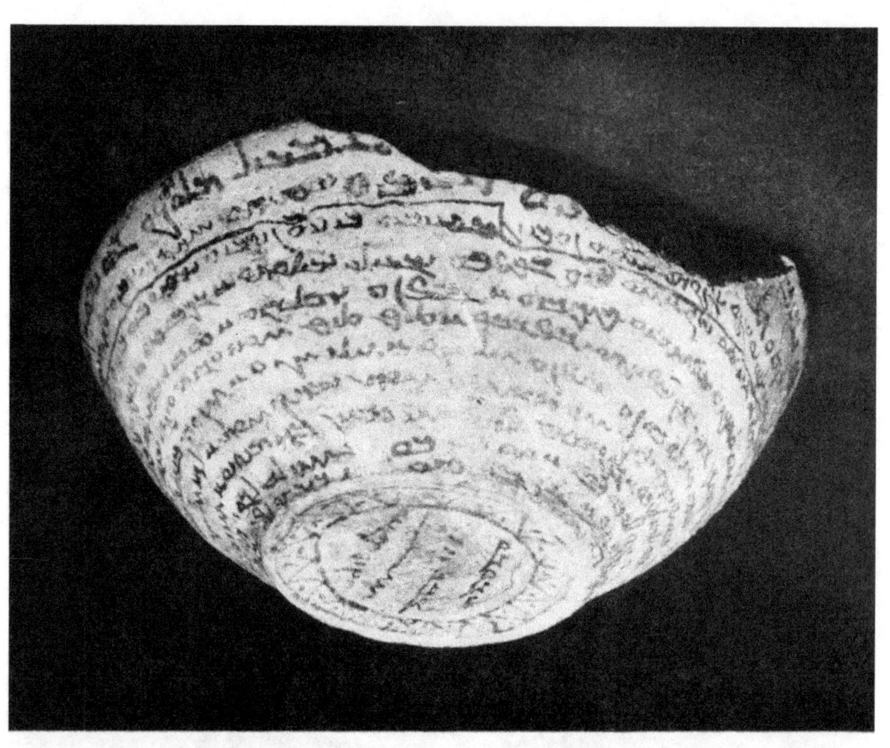

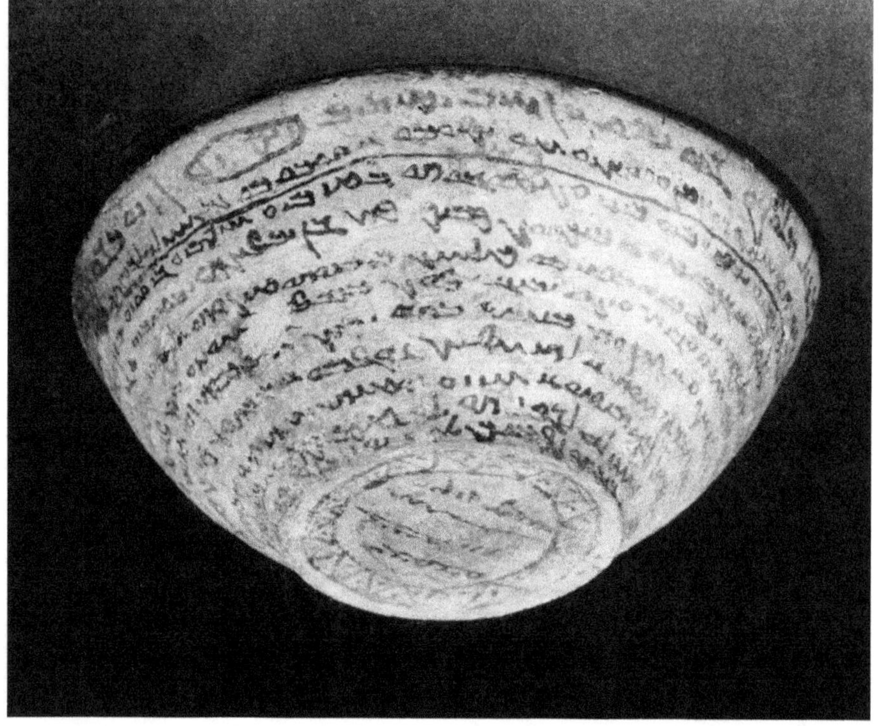

חאילא ד דאיוא מן דיקתא עסיר דורא מן (8) שומיא
עסירא (יא) דיריא ד רוחא ועיארקא ועסיריא
מלאכיא ד באבא (יא) ד רקיחא עסיריא ופכיריא
(9) גדפאירן ד מרכבאתא ד נורא ד יאתביבחין
(חתימא) עסירא דוכתאנא פראוך (פת בזורגאנתאי)
מן יאמינא לעסמלא מן סמלא (10) ליאמינא מן
זימתא ד בריש ואלמא טופריא ד בליגרא (מן
טופריא ד בליגרא ואלמא לזימתא ד ברישא) / /
ימינא לאינא ד סמלא (11) מן (עידנא) עידנא ד
ימינא לעידנא ד ד עסמלא ומן עידנא (ד) סמלא
(ד יאמין) לעידנא / / ולמישמא (12)
עסירא חתימא חזין בישימתא ד דוכתאן פרוך פת
בזורג/ /רקא || (13) ד ארקא (14) עביא
בשירשורא ובזרז/ /נורעיל מלאכא (ת) בשומא
ד זחיר (סיד) וסימיר .ו..י. זיוא רבא
קימאית ובר (15) חייא ו..א.י. בידמיא חא/
/יא .. יריא אסותא וחתמתא וזרזאתא וניאחא
ונטארא ד שרארא נעחוילא לבאיתא דורא וביניאנא
ד (16) דוכתאנפרוך פת בזרגונתאי ולזאוא ובנא
ובנאתא וחייא זאכין עסיריא דיריא זיכריא
ועסיריא דיריא נוקאבאתא עסיריא חילמיא בישיא
וראזיא בישיא (17) וכולחין דמואתא סינאתא ד
חישוכא ד חאגיא בפגרא ובעולא ועולאתא ד
בכראסא ד דוכתאן פרוך פת בזורגונתאי עסיריא
..וחריא (18) בישיא ועדאניא חאשכיא עסיריא
כוכביא ד רגזא ומלאכיא ד קיריא עסירא כולחין
דמואתא סינאתא ד חישוכא לבאר מן (19) פגרא ד
דוכתאן פרוך בת בזורגונתאי בגברא ד אליף אליף
חאויא בית אינא ורובגאן רובגאן חאויא בית
גבינא (בא) (20) ,..אק בחאק ודאק חילא ראזא

ורוגזא חליצא ד̲ חליציא ד̲ חזאת רוחא עמאיכון
חאקאת זאחאת (21) ועתזיחאת רוחא עמאיכון
חאקאת זאחאת ועתזיחאת ד̲ לתיחסון בפגרא ד̲
דוכתאן פרוך פת (22) בזורגונאתאי לעולא דא ד̲
בכראסא עתאחיקון בנימוסא ד̲ חייא ואסותא
וחתמתא וזרזאתא (23) וניאחא ובאסארא רבא ד̲
שרארא בעחוילא̲ לבאיתא ולעסקופתא ד̲
דוכתאנפרוך (24) ולולא ולולאתא ד̲ בכראסא ד̲
דוכתאנפרוך ולזאורא ... (25) ולבנא ולבנאתא
וחייא זאכין (26) ד̲ באבא בראייא חו חזין כסא

Translation

Words in parentheses are superscript.
The break in the bowl is indicated by -BR-.

INTERIOR

(1) In the name of Life! . . . . (2) let healing be to Duktan Pruk, daughter of (3) Bzurgantai; bound are the houses of Sheol with the secret spell 'ZL'WY (4) TYHYN; bound are the dead bones; bound are the swords, the scimitars; (5) checked(?) are the blemishes of the enemies; bound is the boisterous wind of the house of Ptahil; tied are (6) the five angels of this world; bound is Hurmiṣ the sorcery-spirit under (7) the lower waters and the upper waters; bound is the power of the demon by . . . . ; bound is her dwelling by (8) the names; bound are the demons of Ruha (and I shall drive her away) and bound are the angels of the gates of the firmament; bound and tied are (9) the wings of the chariots of fire in which they dwell; (sealed) bound is Duktana Prauk (daughter of Bzurgantai) from the right hand to the left hand, from the left hand (10) to the right hand, from the hair which is on the head and unto the toe-nails which are on the foot (from the toe-nails which are on the foot and unto the hair which is on the head) -BR- the right hand to the eye of the left hand, (11) from the time (the time) of the right hand to the time of the left hand, and from the time of the left hand (of the right hand) to the time -BR- and to hear and to obey; (12) bound, sealed is this soul of Duktan Pruk, daughter of Bzurg -BR- . . . .

EXTERIOR

(13) of the earth; (14) strengthened with the rope and with the girding -BR- Nurel the angel; in the name of Zhir and Smir (. . . . .) the great splendour I have bound; and the Son of (15) Life . . . . he will be silent -BR- . . . . ; let the healing and the sealing and the girding and the refreshment and the safeguard of soundness be to the house, the dwelling, and the building of (16) Duktan Pruk, daughter of Bzrguntai, and to the spouse and the sons and the daughters. And Life is victorious! [*Line around bowl*] Bound are the male demons and bound are the female demons; bound are the evil dreams and the evil secret spells (17) and all the hateful effigies of the darkness which scheme against the body and against the male foetus and the female foetus that are in the womb of Duktan Pruk, daughter of Bzurguntai; bound are the evil . . . . (18) and the dark times; bound are the stars of anger and the angels of strife; bound are all the hateful effigies of the darkness outside of (19) the body of Duktan Pruk, daughter of Bzurguntai; by the Being between whose eyes are a thousand times a thousand beings, and between whose eyebrows are ten thousand times ten thousand beings (in him); (20) . . . . . . Bhaq and has crushed the power, the secret spell, and the anger; the Most Valiant One whom Ruha your mother beheld; she was afraid, she trembled, (21) and she was utterly shaken; Ruha your mother was afraid, she trembled, and she was utterly shaken, so that you [pl.] shall not injure the body of Duktan Pruk, daughter of (22) Bzurgunatai, or this foetus that is in the womb. Be pent in [pl.] by the Law of Life! And the healing and the sealing and the girding (23) and the refreshment and the great safeguard of soundness be to the house and to the threshold of Duktan Pruk (24) and to the male foetus and to the female foetus that are in the womb of Duktan Pruk, and to her spouse . . . . (25) and to the sons and to the daughters. And Life is victorious!

EXTERIOR—BOTTOM OF BOWL

(26) Of the outer gate is this bowl.

Commentary

On the interior, at the bottom of the bowl, a rough circle has been drawn (cf. the first note on Text B); such a circle was seemingly a convention among bowl-writers. Nearly all the Mandaean incantations published display an empty circle, although two of Pognon's texts have a circle with dots in it (IMCK, bowls 6, 17) while in one of Lidzbarski's texts there is the rough figure of a man (MZ, p. 102). It is therefore curious to find in Text D in this study a circle with a cross within it. It is the Jewish bowls that seem to develop the circle theme (see AIT, bowls 7, 31; AMMB, text K). For further variations of the magic circle in the Muslim period, see the Persian amulet reproduced by Budge.[1]

1. *In the name of Life!*: this or a similar phrase occurs at the beginning of a number of Mandaean bowls (e.g., IMCK, p. 25; AIT, p. 252; AMMB, p. 103). "In the name of the Great Life" is very common in the Ginza, especially at the opening of the sections. "Life," in Drower's words, is a "personification of the creative and sustaining force of the universe."[2]

1–2. After the word "Life" there is some confusion in a space for two five-letter words. It is impossible to restore the first word, but the second is probably ʿSWTʾ, a form of ʾSWTʾ (MD, p. 28). ʿSWTʾ is the incantation in its therapeutic function, and the correct translation is "healing" or "remedy" (so MD, p. 28), although Montgomery and Gordon prefer "health" (AIT, p. 248; AMMB, p. 102).

2. *Duktan* is spelled in more than one way in this bowl, but the commonest form is DWKTʾN. This name goes back to the Pers. *dukht*, "daughter" (so MD, p. 104). It appears as a p.n. in other Mandaean bowls: as "Duktanba" in ICGM (p. 206) and as "Duktanush" in IMCK (p. 61), MZ (p. 100), AMMB (p. 98). We may compare the Syr. p.n. DWKT.[3] "Dukht" is a very common element in Persian names (Justi, pp. 86–87, 492–3).

Pruk is derived from the Pers. *farrukh*, "beautiful-faced," "happy," "fortunate"; for its appearance in Persian names, see Justi, pp. 94–97, 493. It is found in other incantations: as plain "Pruk" in an Aramaic bowl (AIT, p. 139); in various combinations in Mandaean sources, "Prukiru" (IMCK, p. 76), "Prukan" (MZ, p. 90), and "Pruksrua" (MZ, p. 100). In these four instances, as in MD, p. 363, it is the name of a male. It also appears as an element in Syriac names.[4]

3. *Bzurgantai*: of the four vocalizations of this word found in our text, the commonest is BZWRGWNTʾY (l. 17). The derivation is Pers.; cf. *buzurg*, "magnificent," "grand," and *buzurgana*, "magnificent," etc. On Persian names with this element in them, see Justi, pp. 359–60 (under "Wazrka"). For the frequency of names ending in ʾY in Mandaic, see MS, pp. 98–99. The sex of Bzurgantai remains in doubt, although probably it

[1]AS, plate VI.
[2]MII, p. xxi.
[3]J. P. Margoliouth, *Supplement to the Thesaurus Syriacus of R. Payne Smith* (Oxford, 1927), p. 84.
[4]Margoliouth, *ibid.*, pp. 274, 276.

is feminine. Matronymic genealogy is the general practice in all the incantation bowls,[5] and Gordon maintains that this usage can be traced back to Seleucid times in Mesopotamia.[6] Drower reports that among modern Mandaeans the mother's name is more important than the father's.[7]

Bound (ʿSYRYʾʾ): the final Aleph evidently replaces the smudged Aleph immediately before it. This form, the emphatic pl. of the p. part., exemplifies the rather loose syntax of the bowl's language. The predicate adjective in Mandaic is usually in the absolute, and this is sometimes adhered to in our present text. Oftener, however, our writer uses the emphatic for the predicate adjective, as in the present instance.

The houses of Sheol is a peculiar phrase and seems to be found nowhere else. Even the term "Sheol" does not appear in any of the other published Mandaean bowls. It is found, however, in the Ginza, where it is a region associated with Darkness (G, p. 270, l. 19), and therefore opposed to the Realm of Light (G, p. 588, l. 24), and the entrance to which is by a gate (G, p. 548, l. 11). Pallis claims that Sheol is the equivalent of the earlier Realm of Darkness, and that the term entered Mandaic through Christian sources, not Jewish.[8] Certainly the Mandaic spelling (ʿŠYWL, ŠYWL) favours its derivation from the Syriac ŠYWL. In the Book of John Sheol clearly designates the world of the dead (J, p. 61, l. 6; p. 113, ll. 6–15). The ordinary Mandaean view is that after death the soul has to pass through a number of posts or stations, *maṭarata* (s. *maṭarta*), before it reaches the scales of judgment, but there is uncertainty in the Mandaean tradition regarding their precise number.[9] *Maṭarata* serve as places of purification for the soul proceeding towards the Realm of Life, and each is in charge of a keeper or keepers. Possibly "the houses of Sheol" may simply mean *maṭarata.*

Secret spell: RʾZʾ ("secret") used here and in ll. 16, 20 apparently designates a spell brought on by a secret formula.

3–4. *ʿZLʿWY TYHYN*: this reading is uncertain. The first word may be related to ʿZLʾ, "web"; the second one is probably "you (pl.) will be." The combination may mean: "Ensnared shall you be." Whatever its meaning, the phrase probably constitutes the aforementioned secret spell.

4. *Dead bones* is doubtless a reference to corpses. Among modern Mandaeans pollution is believed to be caused by contact with the dead,

[5]AIT, p. 49.
[6]AIC, p. 109.
[7]MII, pp. 26, 81.
[8]MS, p. 122.
[9]MS, p. 78f.

and corpses may be abused by evil spirits.[10] Perhaps both of these dangers are here being guarded against.

The swords, the scimitars: I note that in an Aramaic bowl these two words occur together (AIT, bowl 37, l. 8), and in MD (pp. 147, 329) this is said to be frequent in Mandaean exorcisms. In the Ginza the sword is associated with Ruha, Christ, and the Twelve Stars, all of them being looked upon as evil (G, p. 316, ll. 38f.).

5. The first word in this line almost defies identification, and the reading P'YG is largely conjectural. We may have some form of the Pa. of PWG ("check," "enfeeble").

Blemishes: MWMY' can be "oaths," "curses" (as in J.Aram.), but it seems better to take it as "blemishes" (with cognates in B.Heb., Syr., etc.) with MD (p. 261).

Enemies: BYDB'BY' is probably an error for BYLDB'BY'. While there are various spellings of this word (IMCK, p. 258; MD, p. 60), there is no other example of one with a dropped L. It is not clear whether the reference is to human adversaries or demonic ones. Montgomery takes this word to designate a class of demons.[11] In Syr. the singular can refer to the Devil.[12]

Boisterous wind of the house of Ptahil: in the Ginza the wind is associated with Darkness (G, p. 200, ll. 38–41). The phrase "the four winds of the house" occurs several times in the Ginza and in the Book of John; in this context "house" means the terrestrial world (G, p. 15, note 6; cf. MD, p. 47). Our words, "the house of Ptahil," appear in the Ginza (G, p. 358, l. 15; p. 556, ll. 3–5).

Ptahil (usually in Mand. PT'HYL) is a demiurge whose role in Mandaean thought is somewhat ambiguous.[13] There is ascribed to him in the Ginza the creation of the terrestrial world (G, p. 34, l. 1; cf. MII, p. 73), and this suggests that he is opposed to Light. Another part of the Ginza, however, represents him apparently as being reconciled to Life (G, p. 530, ll. 29f.), while elsewhere he seems to be the keeper of one of the *maṭarata* (G, p. 326, l. 16; cf. MS, pp. 78–79). Among modern Mandaeans, Ptahil receives the souls of the dead prior to their passage through the *maṭarata*.[14] Lidzbarski connected the name Ptahil with the Egyptian Ptah (J, p. xxvii, ll. 25f.; cf. MD, p. 384).[15]

[10]MII, pp. 41, 46, 359–60, 362.
[11]AIT, p. 284.
[12]As in the New Testament; e.g., Matt. 10:25.
[13]MII, p. 95.
[14]MII, p. 197.
[15]For another view, which associates the name with PTḤ ("open," "create"), see C. H. Kraeling in *JAOS*, vol. 53 (1933), pp. 152–65.

6. *Five angels of this world* is a reference to the spirits who inhabit or control the five planets and who exercise a malevolent influence over this world. "The five" are referred to in the Ginza (e.g., G, p. 13, l. 27; p. 106, l. 20), and it may be assumed that these are the five planets known to ancient astronomy, excluding the sun and the moon. In the Ginza the planets are represented as the creation of Ruha (on "Ruha," see the note below on l. 8), and therefore as evil (G, p. 99, ll. 19–22; cf. MS, p. 32). "Angel" is used in this bowl, as in the other texts in this study, for either a good or a bad being, and this is the usage of the Ginza (see G, p. 4, ll. 20f.; cf. MD, p. 243). Among modern Mandaeans, however, "angels" are malevolent beings distinguished from "kings" (M'LKY'), who are kindly.[16] For the identification of the seven planets with seven angels, see G, p. 46. l. 29f.

Hurmiṣ (HWRMYṢ): the text may possibly be HYRMYṢ. (a) This could be Mand. for the Greek Hermes, although the commonest forms of Hermes in J.Aram. are 'RMYS, 'RMS', 'YRMYS, HRMYS, HYRMYS, (AIT, p. 123). (b) This may be a form of Ohrmazd (of Zoroastrianism); in J.Aram. this appears as HWRMYZ. MD (p. 138) records the rather rare appearance of HWRMYṢ 'L'H', "the god Hurmiṣ." Hirmiz, Hurmiz, Hurmiṣ are popular names among modern Mandaeans.[17]

Sorcery-spirit (SHR'): the cognates in Akkadian and Arabic support the meaning "sorcery-spirit" (so AIT, p. 248), but Mandaean usage favours "demon" (MD, p. 310). I am using "sorcery-spirit" to differentiate it in translation from D'YW'. The s. of this word is uncommon, although examples of it are found in G, p. 30, l. 15; J, p. 193, l. 14; Q, p. 22, l. 8.

7. *Lower . . . and upper waters*: the usual Mandaean distinction between waters is between "living" or "flowing" water and "black" or "troubled" water; the former belongs to Light, and the latter to earth and Darkness. In the Ginza, however, there is a passage which Lidzbarski renders: "die oberen Wasserquellen vom Himmel and die unteren Wasserquellen von der Erde" (G, p. 409, ll. 8–10); probably it is this distinction which lies behind the language of our bowl. The upper waters may be the living waters of the celestial sphere, the Great Jordan of Life (cf. "the heaven of water" in G, p. 34, l. 1), and the lower waters are the living waters of the terrestrial sphere.

DYQT': the reading and meaning of this word are quite uncertain. MD (p. 108) records DYQ'T', "visions," "appearances," but such a meaning is inappropriate here. We may have the f. p. part. Pe. of DWQ I (MD, p. 105), "the looked-at one," "the venerated one"; this could be an oblique reference to Libat, i.e. Venus.[18]

[16]MII, pp. 27, 94.
[17]MII, p. xxiii, and cf. MD, p. 138.
[18]Cf. MII, pp. 79–80.

8. *Names*: Montgomery summarizes the facts about the magical use of names in AIT, pp. 56f. What is less common is that here, as in Text D, l. 17, no specific names are mentioned. Perhaps it was felt by the bowl-writer that justice could not be done, in the space he had, to the plethora of names available. In the Ginza, for instance, no less than 360 names are ascribed to Jattir-Jathrun, a Light spirit (G, p. 146, l. 18). In one of Montgomery's Aramaic bowls we have: "And all blast-demons and evil-injurers, whose names are recorded in this bowl and whose names are not recorded in this bowl" (AIT, bowl 14, l. 6).

Demons of Ruha: this is written in a space from which some writing has been imperfectly erased. In orthodox Mandaeanism, Ruha is an evil being, and she and her children, the seven planets, are the chief evil spirits. She is termed the Mother of the World and is sometimes called Nimrus or Namrus, as well as Ewath (see J, p. 62, note 3). Probably Ruha epitomizes Mandaean opposition to a number of other religions, especially those with fertility-cult goddesses. This is evident from the fact that Ruha is often termed the Ruha of Holiness, a phrase doubtless taken over from either the Jews or the Christians. Drower notes that in some Mandaean circles, Ruha is looked upon as a kindly spirit.[19]

And I shall drive her away: this is presumably the 1st per. s. imp. Pa. of ʾRQ, with the 3rd s. suffix: enclosed by a line, it may be a powerful spell.

Angels of the gates of the firmament: the last word in this phrase is not well written, but there is some support for thinking it to be RQYHʾ; "gates" is pl. only because the pl. ending is superscript. In the Ginza the firmament, like the earth, is the creation of evil forces (G, p. 34, l. 1; p. 199, l. 3). In this book there are also references to "the twelve gates" (G, p. 20, l. 8; Lidzbarski claims that these are the foreign, false religions) and to "the gates of darkness" (G, p. 70, l. 34), but "the gates of the firmament" appears to be a unique phrase. "Angels" may refer to the planets or to other beings in charge of the gates.

9. *Wings of the chariots of fire*: we may note that as a secondary meaning of GDPʾ, "wing," MD (p. 74) suggests "sail." The word for "chariot," MRKBTʾ, which MD also renders as "ship," often appears in Mand. as a means of locomotion in the heavenly world: the planets, for instance, are said to sit in chariots (G, p. 176, l. 18; J, p. 76, note 3). As for the notion of a heavenly chariot, there is no cogent reason for favouring a Persian source, as Pallis does.[20] Babylonian and other non-Persian seals indicate that the idea of a deity in a chariot was a familiar one in pre-Christian Mesopotamia,[21] as do various references in the Old

[19]MII, p. 398. [20]MS, p. 123.

[21]W. H. Ward, *The Seal Cylinders of Western Asia* (Washington, 1910), pp. 311–13; H. Frankfort, *Cylinder Seals* (London, 1939), plate xxiia.

Testament.[22] The antipathy here shown to fire suggests that the bowl-writer viewed fire as an evil element. In the classical Mandaean writings, the references to fire may be variously interpreted.[23] The opposition of some Mandaean sources to fire doubtless reflects contacts with Zoroastrianism, which venerated fire as a symbol of Ahura Mazda. We may note that in the baptism ritual of modern Mandaeans, the power of fire is formally denied.[24] It is congruous with this that the tradition pictures Ur, a mighty dragon of the underworld and a parent of the planets, as having a belly in which are found alternately fire and ice.[25] Our present phrase, "chariot of fire," is found at least once in the Ginza (G, p. 47, ll. 16f.); Jesus, an evil personage, is seated in it.

Duktana Prauk: this spelling is found only here, although PR'WK may be merely an error for P'RWK. Duktana is noteworthy for it commences with Ḏ instead of D, indicating that the two characters, written differently, were pronounced alike (MG, p. 92; MD, p. 491; cf. the note on WDZ'DWY' in Text D, l. 11).

9–10. *From the right hand . . . to the hair that is on the head*: this phraseology occurs in a Mandaean bowl published by Pognon (ICGM, p. 208), and part of it in an unpublished exorcism cited in MD, p. 178 (under ṬWPR').

9. *From the right hand to the left hand*: in addition to Pognon's bowl just mentioned, I have noticed only one other incantation which mentions the right and left sides (AIT, bowl 6, l. 10). This interest, however, is very characteristic of Mandaean thought, for the Right is symbolical of Light and the Left of Darkness: hence we have the right and left sides of the Ginza. In the modern ritual for the dead, the Mandaean priest says in one of the prayers, ". . . when ye were supported from the left to the right,"[26] and Drower suggests that the phrase means "from evil to good."[27] In their concern over the right and left, the Mandaeans were probably indebted to the professional jargon of the magicians of pre-Christian Mesopotamia.[28]

11. *Time* ('YDN'): the only spelling of this word recorded in MD (p. 341) is 'D'N', which appears in l. 18 of this text.

From the time of the right hand . . .: this unusual phraseology probably

[22]II Kings 2:11; 6:17; Psalms 68:17 (EV); 104:3.
[23]MS, pp. 93–96.
[24]MII, p. 117.
[25]MII, pp. 253–5.
[26]MII, p. 189; cf. pp. 242, 251.
[27]CPM, p. 61, note 3.
[28]For references to the right and left sides in Akkadian magic, see R. C. Thompson's works: *Semitic Magic* (London, 1908), pp. xxiv, xxviii, lix, 166, 171; DESB, vol. 1, pp. 11, 17; vol. 2, p. 153.

reflects the Mandaean view that some hours, days, and seasons are favourable to men, while others are unfavourable.[29] The present incantation is intended to guard its client at all times, both in a season that is propitious and in one that is unpropitious.

To hear and to obey: the break in the bowl obscures the context of these words.

12. *This* (HZYN): while we would expect the f. demonstrative, the m. is sometimes used as here (MG, p. 411).

13. The inscription on the exterior of the bowl commences with this line.

Of the earth: this phrase may have been intended to ensure that the bowl was properly placed in the ground: it may be the equivalent of "This side down."

14. *Strengthened* ('BY'): the reading is uncertain. The form may be the p. part. Pe. of 'BY, "be thick," "be strong" (cf. ABA I, MD, p. 1).

Rope (ŠYRŠWR'): this word, which does not appear in MD, is given in Jast. (p. 1570), although the commoner J.Aram. form is ŠYŠWR' (with cognates in B.Heb. and Syr.). Probably it is being used here metaphorically with reference to the incantation. For a similar metaphor in other bowls, see AIB, text 6, l. 4; AMB, text E, l. 2.

And with the girding: the three lost letters can be restored from ZRZ'T', which appears in ll. 15, 22.

Nurel (NWR'YL) was probably preceded by "in the name of." Nurel and Nuriel (NWRY'YYL) appear in the Ginza (G, p. 173, l. 27), and both are recorded in Schwab (S, p. 296). Nuriel is also found in Aram. incantations (AIT, bowl 35, l. 5; AMB, text B, l. 1).

Zhir (ZHYR) is an *uthra* in the Mandaean tradition (G, p. 221, l. 39). An *uthra* ('WTR') is a heavenly being created for some special purpose, and is always beneficent.[30]

Smir (SYMYR) must be a variant of SMYR who appears in the Ginza as an *uthra* (G, p. 288, l. 23; cf. MD, p. 333). This being is sometimes identified with others, as with Jawar, giving us Jawar-Smir (G, p. 289, l. 1).

SYD: these letters are superscript, between Zhir and Smir, but I can extract no sense from them.

After Smir there appears a word enclosed by a line, but it is only

[29]MII, pp. 74f.

[30]MII, pp. 94–95; M. Lidzbarski, "Uthra und Malakha," in C. Bezold (ed.), *Orientalische Studien, Theodor Nöldeke zum 70sten Geburtstag gewidmet* (Giessen, 1906), pp. 537–45.

partly legible: YWSMYN is a possible reading. This may be a variant of Y'SMYN ("jasmine"), mentioned in the Ginza as "the great Jasmine" (G, p. 116, ll. 13–15).

The great splendour: this may be in apposition to the preceding word. ZYW' ("splendour") occurs in a number of hyphenated names of spirits in the Ginza, e.g., Ham-Ziwa, Jawar-Ziwa, Hibil-Ziwa, Nbat-Ziwa; "the great splendour of Life" appears in G, p. 316, l. 14. ZYW' RB' is recorded as an angel in S, p. 234.

QYM'YT must be 1st per. s. pf. Pe. of QMʿ, "press," "bind," with a cognate in Syr., although we should expect QYMYT or Q'MYT.

14–15. *The Son of Life* (BR HYY'): see the note on this term in J, p. 96, note 2. The expression is applied to the Great Life, especially in the phrase 'BWN BR HYY' (G, p. 220, l. 9); it is also the name of a spirit (G, p. 118, l. 13), and it serves as an epithet for a Mandaean believer, as well as being used as a personal name.

15. *NYDMY'*: the 3rd per. m. s. imp. Pe. of DM'; one meaning of this (not recorded in MD) can be "he will be silent."

. . . *YRY*: the surviving part of one lost consonant suggests that we have here the p. part. m. pl. Pe. of some such verb as KMR ("hide"), QṬR ("tie"), etc.

Healing ('SWT'): a new hand, pen, or ink starts with this word.

Healing and the sealing . . .: this phraseology, with variations, is a stock incantation formula, and is found in the Mandaean bowls hitherto published (cf. Text D, ll. 1–2). These words are echoed in the formula which the modern Mandaean priest pronounces over the navel of a newly born infant. The priest on this occasion presses his "skandola" (a talismanic seal-ring) on the child's navel and says: "In the name of the Great Life! Health and purity, sealing and protection, and the great safeguard of soundness be N's, son of N, etc."[31]

Girding (ZRZ'T'): Drower reports that among modern Mandaeans a small magic roll is called *zrazta.*[32]

Safeguard (NṬ'R'): cf. N'Ṭ'R' found in l. 23. The more usual word is the f. form NṬRT', recorded in MD (p. 282), and found both in Text D (l. 2) and in bowls published by Gordon, Montgomery, and Pognon.

Soundness (ŠR'R') occurs again in l. 23 and also in Text D, l. 2 but it has not appeared in any of the published incantation texts. It is found, however, in Mandaean literature (e.g., G, p. 405, l. 12; p. 521, l. 2), and

[31]MII, pp. 43–44.
[32]MII, pp. 25–26.

it is used in the navel formula quoted a few lines above. For its various shades of meaning, see MD, p. 475.

House . . . dwelling . . . building: this, or a similar, combination of words to describe the home of the exorcist's client is found in other Mandaean inscriptions, including Text D (ll. 2–3) and Text E (l. 2). Possibly this practice is mere verbiage. Most Mandaean homes would consist of one building, a reed or mud-brick hut, which might or might not be large enough to boast a courtyard. Montgomery suggested that in his bowls BYNY'N' means "outbuilding," and perhaps even "cattle-barn" (AIT, p. 245); this would imply that the owner had a higher than average economic position.

16. *Spouse* (Z'W'): for Nöldeke's note on this word, see MG, p. 41, note 6. Like its cognates in J.Aram., Syr., and Arabic, this must be related in some way to the Greek *zeugos*, "team," "pair."

Life is victorious! This is a shortened form of the doxology which appears at the end of many sections and chapters of the Mandaean sacred books, the full wording being: "Life is victorious over all works!" (G, p. 30, l. 26). The shorter form, which is also found in these books (e.g., G, p. 222, l. 34), is very common in CPM, and it appears also in the incantation bowls. Its appearance at this point in our text would seem to indicate the end of the incantation, and this inference is confirmed by the line drawn around the bowl, separating "victorious" from what follows.

16–26. The introduction to this text suggests that these lines were written at a time posterior to ll. 1–15. While the line drawn around the bowl at this point is not the only support for the theory that we have a tripartite text, we should note that in itself the line might merely separate two spells written at the same time, perhaps in the hope that if one failed, the other would work. This is Gordon's explanation of a line on a tablet bearing an Aramaic incantation in cuneiform.[33]

16. *Female demons*: while male demons and various male and female evil spirits are referred to in the published incantations, female demons seem to be referred to only here and in Text D, ll. 8–9.

16–17. *Bound are the evil dreams . . . the darkness*: this phraseology is found, almost verbatim, in ICGM, p. 207.

16. *Dreams*: on the evil source of dreams, see G, p. 5, ll. 24–25.

17. *Hateful* (SYN'T') occurs in the m. s. in Text D, l. 10; the derivation from SN' ("hate") seems clear (see MD, p. 311). Montgomery's view that this word is related to the Syr. SYN' ("dirt"), with an Arabic cognate,

[33]AIC, p. 109.

giving us the meaning "defiling," "foul" (AIT, pp. 251, 296), is improbable.

Effigies (DMW'T'): Montgomery translates this word by "ghosts" (AIT, pp. 82, 248); MD offers "illusory vision" (p. 112) and "spectres" (p. 311, under *saina*).

Darkness (HYŠWK') is normally written HŠWK' in Mand. (MG, p. 118; MD, p. 154), and this appears in Pognon's bowls (IMCK, p. 269). The present orthography seems to be peculiar to the incantations and is found in texts published by both Pognon and Gordon. This reference to darkness reflects the Mandaean view that there is a conflict in this present world between the King of the Light and the King of the Darkness.

Scheme (H'GY'): this somewhat uncertain reading is taken to be the a. part. pl. of HG'. For the ending Y' as indicating both the m. and f. pl., see MG, pp. 165, 268.

Female foetus ('WL'T') is not recorded in MD.

Womb (KR'S'): the usual orthography of this word is KR'S (absolute) and K'RS' (emphatic) (MG, pp. 100, 151; MD, p. 201).

18. At the beginning of this line, and for a space of about three words, there are some marks on the bowl, the remains of an imperfect erasure.

Dark times probably means unfavourable moments and hours; see the note on "the time of the right hand" in l. 11 above, and cf. the modern Mandaean practice of dividing the day into twelve light hours and twelve dark hours.[34]

Stars of anger (there is a small hole in the bowl just before the R of RGZ'): the usual orthography for "anger" is RWGZ', and this is found, although faintly, in l. 20. The present phrase appears in the Ginza in association with Kewan (Saturn) (G, p. 223 l. 22), and this makes it probable that in our present text "stars" designates "planets," as is often the case in the Ginza (e.g., G, p. 13, l. 27). Our phrase probably means "angry stars," or, if we give RWGZ' a meaning it sometimes has in J.Aram., "stars of trouble," i.e., stars causing trouble. I note that the expression "angels of anger" appears in Q, p. 131, l. 2; for a similar phrase, see Text E, l. 16.

Angels of strife: these are malevolent angels, as in l. 6. This phrase occurs in one of Montgomery's Mandaean bowls (AIT, bowl 39, l. 7); his facsimile of the text (AIT, plate xxxv) indicates, however, that his reading is erroneous, and that we should read KWKBY' D̲ RWGZ' WML'KY' D̲ QYRY'. This correction was made by Epstein, although

[34]MII, pp. 74, 75, 81.

he wrongly retained Montgomery's reading of the first word as WRWRBY' (GBA II, p. 61); cf. MIT, pp. 347–8.

19. *By the Being*: for the various meanings of GBR', see MD, p. 73. The reference here is apparently to some angelic being, but his identity is obscure. The description of him which follows is, as far as I know, unique, although it has affinities with the portrayal of Shar, an *uthra*, in one of de Morgan's inscriptions cited by Lidzbarski (J, p. 6, note 2).

Between whose eyes: for BYT meaning "between," see MG, p. 194; MD, p. 64. The form 'NY̱' can be either s. or pl., with suffix (MG, p. 178).

Ten thousand . . . beings: RWBG'N is an anomalous form; the recognized orthography of this word is RWB'N (MG, p. 190). The use of thousand and ten thousand is a common Mandaean method of indicating a superlative quantity (e.g., G, p. 66, l. 3; p. 195, l. 10). H'WY' is taken to be the a. part. pl. Pe. of HW', with the meaning "beings."

20. *In him* (B'): I cannot determine the significance of these superscript letters. They may have some connection with the next word, which is smudged.

Bhaq, sometimes Bhaq-Ziwa, appears in Mandaean literature as one who calls himself the Father of the *uthras* (G, p. 76, l. 30; p. 97, l. 21; etc.). BHQ ZYW' appears as a Jewish angel in S, p. 193. It will be noted that the words before and after Bhaq each end in 'Q: this assonance may have been thought to contribute to the efficacy of the incantation.

The Most Valiant One (HLYṢ' Ḏ HLYṢY'): this seems to describe some august Mandaean heavenly being.

Ruha your mother: note the use with a s. noun of a suffix normally used with a pl. (MG, p. 180). The antecedent of this suffix is presumably all the evil powers mentioned in the previous lines.

20–21. *She was afraid . . . utterly shaken*: cf. a Mandaean hymn used on Sundays, in which the following occurs: H'Q'T WZ'H'T N'MRWS, which Lidzbarski translates: "Namrus fürchtete und ängstigte sich" (Q, p. 184, l. 9 of the Mandaic text). As indicated earlier (note on l. 8 above), Namrus is one of the names of Ruha.

20. *H'Q'T* ("she was afraid") is the 3rd per. f. s. pf. Pe. of HUQ, 'UQ (MD, p. 137).

Z'H'T ("she trembled") is the pf. Pe. of ZW', ZWH (MD, pp. 162, 164).

21. *'TZYH'T* ("she was utterly shaken") is probably the defective writing of the Etta. of the same root, ZWH.

So that you shall not injure (D̲ LTYHṬWN): D̲ is taken as a conjunction (MG, p. 461). LTYHṬWN must be equivalent to L' TYHṬWN. L' sometimes loses its vowel to the following word, but usually only when the word has an initial vowel (MG, pp. 35, 203). This same verb, HṬ', is used in Pognon's bowls to describe the activities of demons (IMCK, bowls 22, 23, pp. 62, 67, 266).

22. *This foetus* (L'WL' D'): the initial L apparently indicates the object of the preceding "injure." As 'WL' is m., the use of D', a rare f. demonstrative (MG, p. 89; MD, p. 97), is unexpected. Alternatively, D may be an error for T, in which case we would really have 'WL'T' as in l. 17.

Be pent in ('T'HYQWN): the first and third letters are almost illegible. I am taking the word, with some hesitation, to be an Etta. form (not mentioned in MD, p. 137) of 'WQ. It can be either the 2nd per. pl. pf., or the 2nd pl. imv. The meaning "be pent in" is supported by Syr. and J.Aram.; the commoner meaning in Mand. would be "be terrified."

Law (NYMWS'), like its Semitic cognates, is clearly a borrowing from the Greek *nomos*. On its various meanings, see G, p. 248, note 3; MD, p. 298.

23. *Threshold* ('SQWPT'): this is perhaps the commonest form of this word (MG, p. 46, note 4), but variations in the orthography do appear (MD, p. 335, under *squpta*). In one of Lidzbarski's texts we find 'SKWPT' (MZ, bowl AO 2629, p. 102), which is in fact identical with the Syr. cognate. Drower notes that among the modern Mandaeans the threshold is of great importance and is protected by charms.[35]

24. *And to the male foetus* (WLWL'): this word and the next one illustrate the loss of initial ' after the preposition (MG, p. 71). That this loss does not always occur is shown by L'WL' in l. 22 and WL'SQWPT' in l. 23.

Spouse: after this word there are about eight or ten letters, but some are almost illegible, and I am unable to attach any meaning to them. We might expect them to constitute the name of the husband.

26. *Of the outer gate*: these and three other words ("is this bowl") are written in four short lines on the exterior of the flat base of the bowl, and are encircled by a decorative border. The phrase doubtless designates the particular spot where the bowl was deposited. For similar instructions in other bowls, cf. IMCK, bowl 8 and AMMB, text M.

[35]MII, p. 50.

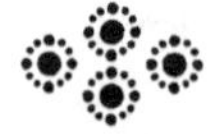

BOWL D (931.4.2)

Introduction

THIS BOWL, like that with Text C, was purchased in Baghdad in 1931 by Professor T. J. Meek of the University of Toronto. Its provenance was given as Kammaz (on the left bank of the Tigris, near Baghdad). It is a poorly made bowl of medium ware with a flat base. It has numerous grits, although these are partly obscured by the creamish slip. Its dimensions are: height, 8.4 cm.; diameter at top, 20.7 cm.; diameter at base, 7 cm.; thickness, 0.5 cm. There are no marks on the outside of the bowl, but on the inside there is a long inscription in Mandaic. The bowl itself is in an almost perfect state of preservation, the two lacunae in the last line of the text, caused by small chips at the bowl's edge, being readily supplied from the context.

The inscription was written to protect Buktuya, son of Kushai, and his wife Zaduya, daughter of Shirin, and their household from the machinations of various evil beings. One writer appears to have been responsible for the entire incantation. There is no hint of any special circumstances that led to the production of our text, except that ll. 9–11 and 13–15 imply that malicious spirits are actually at work in the family, their presence being evidenced, doubtless, by sickness or misfortune.

Since the language of the bowl is Mandaic, it is a natural inference that the persons for whom it was written were Mandaeans. Even though they were illiterate Mandaeans, it may have been a comfort to them to know that the incantation was in the language of their sacred books. We cannot, however, be at all certain about the identity of the charm-writer, to whose discretion would probably be left the general character and content of the incantation itself. Had this person been a Mandaean, we should have expected his vocabulary to reflect that fact. But a feature of our text (though one shared by other Mandaic bowls, e.g., bowls 38 and 39 in AIT) is that it is almost completely devoid of the Mandaean religious jargon; as the notes indicate, connections with the ideas of classical Mandaean literature are few and unimportant. Even the numerous angelic host of Mandaeanism is almost completely overlooked, Gabriel being the only member of that company to find a place in the inscription (l. 9). Angels are not forgotten in our text, but most of those mentioned appear to be Jewish angels. This fact, along with a limited number of other words familiar to us from Jewish sources, suggests that the bowl-writer, if a Mandaean, was strongly influenced by Jewish ideas and Jewish magic. Such influence could easily have been felt in pre-Islamic Mesopotamia where syncretism in religion and magic was widespread. Another possibility is that this text was written by a Jewish magician who was versatile enough to know Mandaic.

A striking feature of this text is the appearance in l. 15 of a series of signs, sixty-three in number, extending a little over half way around the bowl; three others appear in l. 17. These signs are presumably of a magical character. Most of them are actually letters of the Mandaic alphabet, written either singly or in meaningless groups; the rest are non-alphabetic. Nonsense words have already been commented on in Text B, l. 2. Magic symbols are familiar phenomena in Egyptian and Greek magical papyri and on Gnostic amulets, but they are uncommon in the magic bowls. Some appear in a bowl which is used as an illustration opposite p. 447 in H. V. Hilprecht, *The Excavations in Assyria and Babylonia* (Philadelphia, 1904); this bowl, as far as I know, has never been fully studied. Another bowl, with a Syriac text published by Gordon, contains five magic signs in ll. 1, 14, 16 (IES). While it seems impossible to track down most of the signs in our present text to their place and date of origin, some of them appear to have affinities with Egyptian and Greek symbolism. They belong, as it were, to the international world of magic. It may be suspected that the Babylonian Jews, through their various connections with the Mediterranean area, were more closely in touch with these broader aspects of magic than were the more provincial Mandaeans. The presence of these symbols in our text may therefore be further evidence of Jewish influence in its composition.

Text

// indicates a chip at the edge of the bowl.

(1) אסארא וסותא וחתאמתא וזרתא (2) ונטרתא

רבתיא ב̱ שרארא תחילא̱ לבאיתא דורא̱ (3) וחיכלא

וביניאנא ולחמא ומיא ולעקופתא כולא ד בוכתיא
ברכושאי (4) ולזאוא זאדויא בתשירין ולאכול
אנאשיא באיתא משבנא עליכון אסאריא בריאתא
כולחון (5) חזא ומחזא בשום. איל יח יח
יח. יח יח יח יח קאדוש מלכותא ובשומא ד
(6) מיסטרון חלדח ד חו משאמיש קדים ברגודא
וחו רחים על מאדא וחו ראחים על באריא חו מימיא
על (7) אכדוראניא מלאכיא מאותא ד חאלאחכין ד
חליא ביסרא למיכאל וחמרא למישתיא קאל זינא
וצוחתא וצוחתא ומצותא קאל רבא ד דיויא(8)בישיא
ודיויא טאביא שידיא פיגיא ולא טאביא ולילייאתא
ודיויא חוראייא ודיויא אארמאייא ומלאכיא
פרסאייא ומלאכיא חוזאייא ודיויא זיכריא
ודיויא (9) נוקבאתא אנאתון שבתון ומבטלין
אריתון מן באיתא ד בוכתויא ברכושאי ומן זאוא
זאדויא בת שירין ומן כולחון אנאשיא באיתא בשום
גבריאייל (10) מיכיאיל מלאכיא וזיאיל מלאכא
בשום נדריאיל מלאכא בשום יחדיאיל מלאכא אנאתון
מלאכיא תיבטלון כול מידים סאינא מן באיתא ד
בוכתויא ברכושאי ומן זאוא זאדויא (11) בת
שירין ומן מדורתא ומן בנא ומן בנאתא ד
בוכתויא בר כושאי ודזאדויא בחשירין ומן קיניאנא
ומן כול ביסרא וזמא ד אית בחאחו באיתא ד
בוכתויא ברכושאי ודזאדויא בת שירין (12) בשום
אדרבאן ארוחון אמין משח רבותא אנא אנא משח
כמא ד חיאיל ד חאיל וזיויאיל זיוא וחדריאיל
חדרא לביש וחסדיאיל חסדא לביש בשום אדרבאן
אדרבאן תקיף (13) חוס פס גאס וקמיאייל רבא
אנתון כול אתגיא אנתב. אייר ד יאבא על שובא
רק.. עלאייא ופריאיל אנתון אנת וחאלין מלאכיא

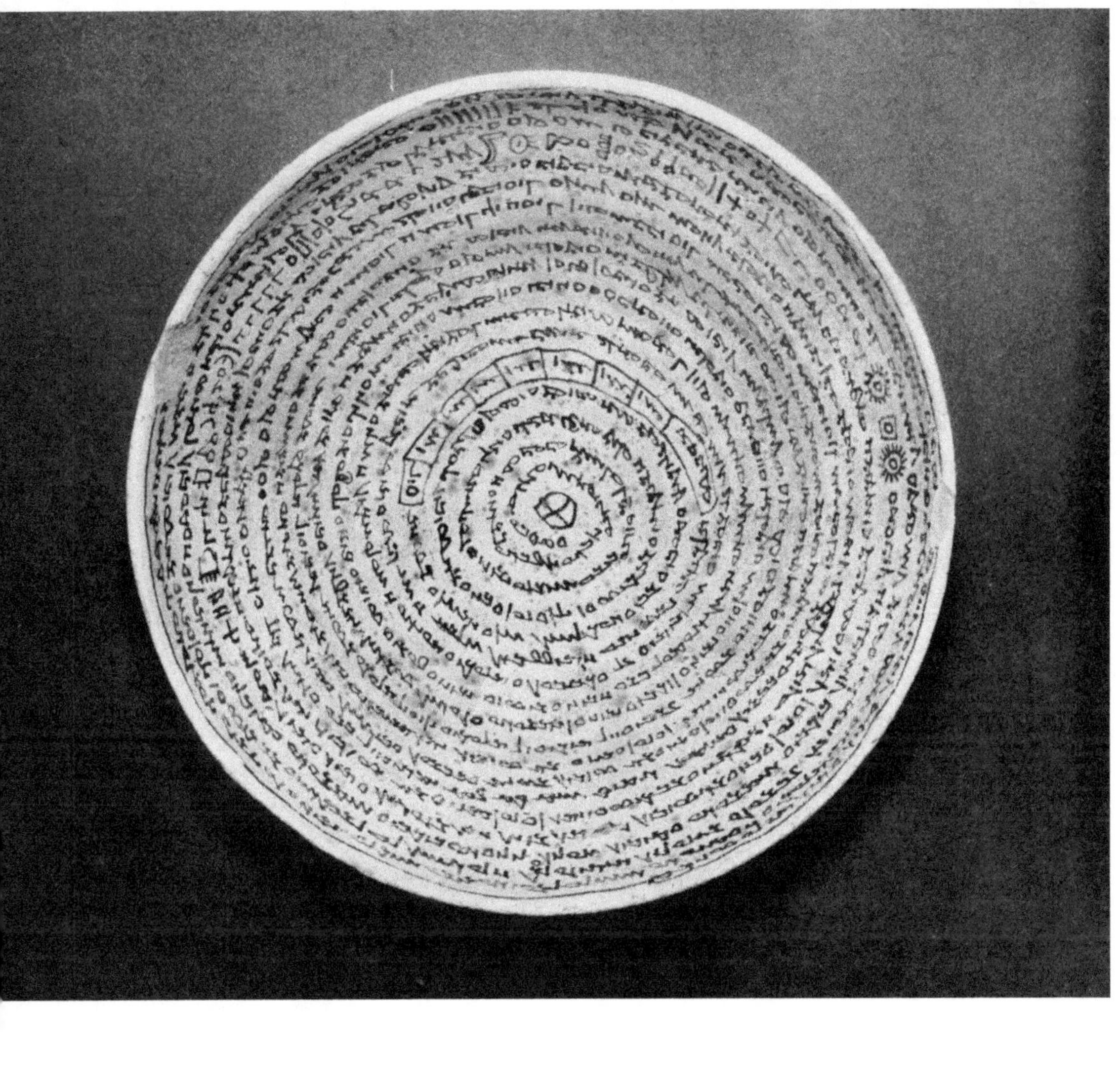

ד כתיבינבא בכאסא חאדין ליבטולין מינא ד
בוכתויא ברכושאי ומן (14) זאוא זאדויא בת
שירין ומן באיתא ד בוכתויא ברכושאי ומן זאדויא
בת שירין כול סטאניא בישיא דיכריא ונוקבאתא מן
באיתא ומן אסקופתא ד בוכתויא ברכושאי ומן זאוא
זאדויא בתשירין (15) ביון ומן בנאתון אמין
אמין סאלח לו ות וזעא
זוווללא זאזא קקוענון א א
סאזז א ואאססל אסארין ד
כול רוחין דיכריא ונוקבאתא אסירין חאלין (16)
ליליאתא דיכריא ונוקבאתא אסירליא וחתימאליא
ד אסארין לא מישתריא מומינאלך ומשבנאלך מומיא
אנא אח וא דיכרתע מויעין אנאתא וחויא על
אכמאחין אכמאחין בישא ועל קאיען גרבאנא בחאלין
מומינאלאך (17) ד לא תחון לא לבוכתויא
ברכושאי ולאזאדויא בתשירין חבריא בליליא
ולאצאותא באימאמא אזזזזזזז על עזא חלא
נזקם אסארא ואסותא וחתמתא וזרזתא ונטרתא מן
שומיא ומן מלאכיא ד אסואתא תחוילא (18) לבאיתא
דורא וחיכלא וביניאנא ולבנא ולאבנאתא
ולעסקופתא כולא ד / /יא ברכושאי
ומנזאואזאדויא בת שירין ולבנאיון זיכיא
ולבנאתון נוקבאתא ולכולחון אנאש/ /תא איין
ואמין אמין אמין סאלא שלימא

Translation

(1) Let the spell and the healing and the sealing and the girding (2) and the great safeguard of soundness be to the house, the dwelling, (3) and the habitation and the building and the bread and the water, and to all the threshold of Buktuya, son of Kushai, (4) and to the spouse Zaduya, daughter of Shirin, and to all the people of the house; I adjure

on your behalf the spells, all of them created beings (5) . . . . in the name of | El | Yh | Yh | Yh | Yh | Yh | Yh | Yh | Qadosh | the Kingdom, and in the name of (6) Metatron HLDH who serves before the Curtain and who has compassion upon the town and who has compassion upon the countryside; he conjures (7) the hundreds of fierce angels of Halahkin, who has sweetened meat for eating and wine for drinking. The sound of the weapon, and the shout and the shout and the command! The voice of the Master of (8) the evil demons and the good demons, the dumb and no-good devils, and the Liliths, and the Hurrian demons, and the Aramaean demons, and the Persian angels, and the Hozaite angels, and the male demons, (9) and the female demons. Cease (pl.), and frustrated go trembling from the house of Buktuya, son of Kushai, and from the spouse Zaduya, daughter of Shirin, and from all the people of the house. In the name of the angels Gabriel, (10) Michael and the angel Ziel; in the name of the angel Nadriel; in the name of the angel Yhadiel. You angels shall destroy whatsoever is hateful from the house of Buktuya, son of Kushai, and from the spouse Zaduya (11), daughter of Shirin, and from his dwelling and from the sons and from the daughters of Buktuya, son of Kushai, and of Zaduya, daughter of Shirin, and from the possessions and from all the flesh and blood that are in that house of Buktuya, son of Kushai, and of Zaduya, daughter of Shirin. (12) In the name of Adrban Aruhun. Amen Moses of the myriads: I myself am Moses just as much as Hiel who is strength and Ziwiel who is spendour and Hadriel who is clothed with beauty and Hasdiel who is clothed with kindness. In the name of Adrban, mighty Adrban, (13) hasten, vanish, perish, and the great Qmiel Antun all . . . . upon the seven upper firmaments, and Priel Antun you (s.) and these angels who are inscribed in this bowl, let them destroy from (the person of) Buktuya, son of Kushai, and from (14) the spouse Zaduya, daughter of Shirin, and from the house of Buktuya, son of Kushai, and from Ẓaduya, daughter of Shirin, all evil satans male and female, from the house and from the threshold of Buktuya, son of Kushai, and from the spouse Zaduya, daughter of Shirin, and from (15) their sons and from their daughters. Amen Amen Selah. [1]#### LWWT ### WZ‘’ # ZWWWLLL’ # Z’Z’ # QQW‘NWN ### ’ # ’ ### S’ZZ # ’ ## W’’SSL ###. Spells of all male and female spirits. Bound are these (16) male and female Liliths. I have bound and I have sealed with spells which are unbreakable. I conjure you (s.) and I adjure you (s.) with the exorcisms: I am a kinsman and I will invoke a decree and it will guard the (household) vessels. And be (s.) upon Akmahin, the sickly Akmahin, and upon Cain (?) the leper. By these I conjure you (s.) (17) that you (pl.) may not be to Buktuya, son of

[1]# represents a magic sign.

Kushai, and to Zaduya, daughter of Shirin, comrades in the night and for companionship in the day. 'ZZZZZZZ #. Against the Strong One are there not injuries? Let the spell and the healing and the sealing and the girding and the safeguard of the names and of the angels of healings be (18) to the house, the dwelling, and the habitation, and the building, and to the sons and to the daughters and to all the threshold of Buktuya, son of Kushai, and of (lit. "from") the spouse Zaduya, daughter of Shirin, and to their male sons and to their female daughters, and to all the people of the house. Yea and Amen Amen Selah. Finished.

Commentary

On the cross and circle at the centre of the bowl, see the first note on Text C.

1–2. *Let the spell* . . .: cf. the note on similar phraseology in Text C, l. 15.

1. WSWT' . . . WZRT': cf. W'SWT' . . . WZRZT' in l. 17.

3. *Habitation* is one of the meanings HYKL' has in Mandaic, thus preserving some of the meaning of the Sumerian original, *e-gal*, "great house."

Bread . . . *water*: probably this is a reference to the conventional elements which sustain life. This phrase, apparently with the same sense, occurs in G, p. 21, l. 28. It seems unlikely that there is any allusion to the sacramental elements, bread and water, used by the Mandaeans on various occasions, for these elements cannot be kept overnight.[2]

'*QWPT*' is an error for 'SQWPT', "threshold"; see the note on this word in Text C, l. 23.

Buktuya (BWKTY'): elsewhere in the bowl this appears as BWKTWY'. I cannot find any occurrence of this name outside the present incantation. Mandaean proper names frequently end in WY': e.g., Zaduya (Z'DWY') in the next line, and various names in IMCK, pp. 100–1. Presumably the BWKT element comes from the Pehlavi *būkht*, "freed," "ransomed"; for the use of the latter in Persian names, see Justi, pp. 72, 490.

Kushai (KWŠ'Y): this name does not seem to occur alone elsewhere, although it appears as part of other names: KW'ŠYZ'G in one of Pognon's bowls (ICGM, pp. 207, 222), and KWŠYZ'G in a Lidzbarski text (MZ,

[2]MII, p. 102, 107, 164, 196.

p. 100, note 3). Our word must go back to the Pers. *khuš*, "happy," "good," etc. For the name *Khuši* in Pers. and for Persian names with the element *khuš* in them, see Justi, pp. 180–1, 501.

4. *Zaduya* (Z'DWY') appears as the name of a male three times in published texts: once in a Mand. text (AIT, bowl 38, l. 12) and twice as ZDWY in J.Aram. texts (AIT, bowl 10, l. 5; AMMB, text K, l. 1). It is undoubtedly the Pers. *Zadhoe* or *Zaduyeh* (Justi, p. 378), which presumably is related to *zād*, "birth," "child of."

Shirin (ŠYRYN) occurs as part of a woman's name in a J.Aram text (AIT, bowl 9, l. 4). It is from the Pers. *šīrīn*, "milky," "sweet," "pleasant," which serves also in Pers. as a f. name (Justi, pp. 302–3, 511).

L'KWL: the preposition L is sometimes written L' before nouns (MG, p. 10; MD, p. 226; also later in this text, ll. 17, 18).

The people of ('N'ŠY'): this is to be construed as the cst. pl.; for the ambiguity of the ending Y', see MG, p. 161.

I adjure on your behalf: the full orthography of this a. part. with suffix would be M'ŠB'N'. Usually the preposition which follows this verb, either L or ʿL, indicates the power being invoked (e.g., AIT, bowl 1, l. 8). In our present text the antecedent of "on your behalf" seems to be the objects and persons mentioned in ll. 2–4.

5. *HZ' WMHZ'* are quite legible, but I can make no sense of them. Possibly we have a J.Aram. phrase, written defectively, for HZY WMHZY (p. parts. Pe. and Pa.), "visible and revealed," or we may have the corresponding forms in Mand. (for HZY' WMH'Z'Y) with the same meaning. Against the latter is that MD (p. 139) does not record the Pa. or Aph. of this verb.

El, Yh (7 times) . . . Qadosh: one explanation of these words is that they are intended to strengthen the phrase "in the name of the Kingdom," in the middle of which they are placed. As the words might be thought to be of Jewish origin, this explanation could point to Jewish influence in our text. I note, however, that Drower treats "Ya" in the Mandaean liturgy as merely a magical name (CPM, p. 11, note 4), and also that in a phylactery published by her, the phrase occurs "in the name of the angel Qadushan" (PR, p. 344). A second interpretation of these words is that the bowl-writer wished to curb the malevolent Jewish god, and he therefore placed these Jewish terms in little boxes and enclosed them with the potent phrase "in the name of the Kingdom." It may be observed that in the Ginza, El (also El-El), the Great El, and Qadosh are associated with Ruha and the powers of Darkness (G, p. 25, l. 8; p. 234, l. 15; p. 260, ll. 20, 28).

Kingdom is apparently used here to designate the Realm of the King of Light: it has this sense in both the Ginza and the Qulasta (G, p. 7, l. 8; Q, p. 240, l. 4).

6. *Metatron* (MYṬṬRWN): according to the *Jewish Encyclopaedia* of 1904 (vol. 8, p. 519), this name appears only in Jewish sources. I have noticed it in at least four Aramaic incantations: *Zeitschrift für Assyriologie*, vol. 9 (1894), bowl 2416, pp. 11–27, note 6; AIT, bowl 25; AMMB, text L; AMB, text D. The present instance is the first appearance of Metatron in any published Mandaean material. Its earliest occurrence in Jewish literature is in the Palestinian Midrash on Deuteronomy, which dates from about 150–225 A.D. In the Babylonian Talmud it is the designation of an angel who is numbered among "the angels of the Presence," and who has many of the rights traditionally given to Michael.[3] The appearance of Metatron in our present text supplies further evidence of Jewish influence on the bowl-writer, and it also favours 200–300 A.D. as the *terminus a quo* for this text.

HLDH, of which the last two letters are somewhat uncertain, may be some cryptic name for Metatron. ḤLDH appears as an Aram. p.n. in S. A. Cook, *Glossary of Aramaic Inscriptions* (Cambridge, 1898), p. 53, while ḤLD and ḤLDY are found in B.Heb. (cf. Mand. KLD', "bewitch," MD, p. 216).

QDYM is being taken as the preposition "before," though the usual orthography for this in Mand. is QWD'M (MG, p. 194); cf. QDWM in Text E, l. 7. Jastrow cites QDYM as a variant of QDM (Jast., p. 1315), and in Syr., Brockelmann gives QDYM as a variant of QDM (*Lexicon Syriacum* [Halle, 1928], p. 647).

Curtain (BRGWD'): on this word see MG, p. 47, note 2, and cf. MD, p. 69. In J.Aram. PRGWD' has as one meaning "curtain (of heaven)," which may be pertinent here. The phrase "the great curtain of soundness" occurs at least twice in the Ginza (G, p. 212, l. 8; p. 429, l. 7).

RHYM is defective writing for the fourth next word R'HYM.

Town (M'D'): as M'D', "knowledge," makes no sense here, I assume that this is the J.Aram. (as well as the Syr.) MT'; the only Mand. cognate given for the latter is M'T' (MG, p. 99; MD, p. 256). On the change of Semitic T to D in Mand., see MG, p. 42, though Nöldeke's examples are confined to triliteral words whose middle radical is a T.

B'RY': as B'R does not seem to be used in the pl., I am taking this to be meant either for B'R'Y or for B'R'Y' (MD, p. 50).

[3]For discussions of "Metatron" see: G. F. Moore, *Harvard Theological Review*, vol. 15 (1922), pp. 62–85; M. Black, *Vetus Testamentum*, vol. 1 (1951), pp. 217–19; A. Murtonen, *Vetus Testamentum*, vol. 3 (1953), pp. 409–411.

MYMY' appears to be an error for MWMY'. The latter form, with a personal pronoun, occurs twice in l. 16. The correct form of the a. part. Aph. of YM' is M'WMY' (see MG, p. 246).

7. *Fierce* ('KDWR'NY'), which is not recorded in MD, is probably cognate to the B.Heb. 'KZR, "cruel," "fierce" (with parallels in J.Aram. and Syr.). On D and Z in Mand., see MG, p. 43; on the suffix 'N for forming nouns and adjectives, see MG, p. 135.

Hundreds (M'WT'): neither MG (pp. 189–90) nor MD (p. 238) gives any Mand. pl. for "hundred."

Halahkin (H'L'HKYN) may be the name of some angel; possibly the first part of it has some relation to HLY' which follows. It may, however, be a corruption of 'L'H', "god," a term generally used by the Mandaeans of false foreign deities (G, p. 4, ll. 23–29). In two of Pognon's bowls, "god" has an evil sense (IMCK, bowls 25, 29), whereas in one of Montgomery's Mandaean texts it bears the opposite meaning (AIT, bowl 38, l. 7).

Has sweetened (HLY') is taken to be the Pa. pf. of HL'.

Meat . . . wine: this may be a stock phrase for common food, although among the modern Mandaeans little meat is normally eaten (what is, is mostly mutton), while the wine that is drunk is usually nothing but water flavoured with fruit juice.[4]

The sound of the weapon and the shout . . .: these words must refer to the activities of the beneficent beings; their recital is designed to send the malevolent creatures away trembling.

Weapon (ZYN') is more commonly written Z'YN'.

Shout (ṢWHT'), well known in J.Aram. and Syr., does not appear in MD.

Command (MṢWT'), which is unknown in Syr., does not appear in MD (cf. *mṣuta*, "strife," MD, p. 277).

7–8. *Evil demons . . . good demons*: demons are usually evil in Mandaean thought (e.g., G, p. 28, l. 25), although Drower refers to the *deyvi* (i.e., *daiwia*, "demons") who inhabit the *maṭarata* (see note on "houses of Sheol" in Text C, l. 3), and who offer nourishment to the souls of men after death.[5] Apparently the bowl-writer cannot trust even those demons commonly reckoned to be good.

8. *Dumb* (PYGY') is a term frequently used of demons (MG, p. 39, l. 7; MD, p. 370).

[4]MII, pp. 47–48, 68.
[5]MII, p. 198.

Liliths are female demons, usually malevolent, as in l. 16; on a good Lilith, see MII, p. 46; on Liliths in demonology, see AIT, pp. 75–78; MIT, pp. 37–39.

Hurrian . . . Hozaite: in one of Gordon's Aramaic bowls, there is a somewhat similar list of gentilics: "Aramean . . . Jewish . . . Shiite . . . Persian . . . Indian . . . Greek . . . Roman . . ." (AMB, text D, ll. 8–9).

Hurrian (HWR'YY'): the context and the affix 'YY' suggest that this is either a gentilic or a geographical term. Possibly this is to be related to the B.Heb. ḤRYM ("Horites"), a term used of the early inhabitants of Edom (Deut. 2:12, 22), and which must have reached our bowl-writer (or his tradition) from some Jewish or Christian source. Another possibility is that this word is a legacy from the second millennium B.C., when the historical Hurrians flourished in western Asia (cf. the Hurrian stem, *ḥuru* or *ḥurw*). There may have been some conflation of these two traditions, with the result that Horites and Hurrians were treated as identical. Another explanation of our word is that it means "marsh," being an adjective derived from Mand. H'WRY', "marshes" (MD, p. 117).

Aramaean: there are two Alephs at the beginning of this word, but as the first is smudged, it probably should be ignored. "Aramaean" is not recorded in MD. Montgomery claims that this word is in one of Pognon's bowls (AIT, p. 283), but Pognon's facsimile gives but slight support for this (IMCK, bowl 27). The meaning of Aramaean in our text is not clear. It may refer to the Christian community of Mesopotamia (cf. AMB, text D, p. 30), or to non-Mandaean groups in general (cf. the use in J.Aram. of 'RM'Y to denote "gentile" or "pagan").

Persian: the reference may be to Sasanian Persia or to the Zoroastrianism which flourished at this time. The Ginza has a few references to Persians in pre-Islamic days (G, p. 411, l. 28; p. 416, l. 19); cf. an unpublished magic roll, cited by Drower, in which the following appears: "Come and tread down the kingdom of the Persians and the Medes in the name of the seven mysteries of their father."[6]

Hozaite (HWZ'YY') may come from the J.Aram. ḤWZ'Y or BY ḤWZ'Y, identified as "a district on the caravan road along the Tigris and its canals" (Jast., p. 430); ḤWZ'H is an inhabitant of this district. If this is what our text means, it seems a rather inadequate complement to the preceding "Persian." The Akkadian *Ḫaz-za-na-bi* (a district in western Iran, south of Parsua) appears to be chronologically too remote from our bowl-writer, as well as too restricted geographically. A more attractive possibility is that our word is related to the Pers. *khūz*, ancient Elam, which usually has the longer form *khūzistan*. Against this is the fact that the classical Mand. for Khuzistan is KWZYST'N (MD, p. 206).

[6]MII, p. 18, note 8.

Male (ZYKRY'): with the exception of ZYKY' in l. 18, this word appears elsewhere in this text as DYKRY' (ll. 14, 15, 16). Both spellings appear in MD (pp. 107, 159).

9. *Cease* (ŠBTWN): I assume this to be 2nd per. pl. imv. Pe. of ŠBT ("cease," "rest"), though I note that as the Mand. for "Sabbath" is Š'PT' (MD, p. 444), we should expect the cognate verb, "rest," to be ŠPT, whereas the latter in Mand. means "place," "set" (MD, p. 473). If our identification of this form is correct, it is further evidence of a Jewish influence in our text.

Frustrated (MBṬLYN): the pl. of the p. part. Pa.

Go trembling ('RYTWN): the pl. imv. Aph. of RTT ("tremble"), though the Aph. of this verb is not mentioned in MD (p. 438).

Gabriel: the earliest literary allusion to the angel Gabriel is in a second century B.C. Jewish source (Daniel 8:16); how or when this angel entered Mandaean thought we do not know. The name occurs several times in the Ginza, but there seems to be confusion regarding the personage so designated. He once appears as the creator of the world (G, p. 15, l. 21), but usually he is identified with other beings: with Hibil-Ziwa (G, p. 14, l. 26), and also with Ptahil-Uthra (G, p. 98, l. 11; p. 284, l. 13). He also is found in the Mandaean incantations, but much less frequently than in the Jewish texts (on the latter, see AIT, p. 96).

10. *Michael* (MYKY'YL): in B.Heb. MYK'L. This name was first applied to an angel in the book of Daniel (10:13), and subsequently Michael became in a special sense a Jewish angel, a kind of patron saint and celestial champion of Irael. It is therefore not surprising that the Mandaeans should have left him strictly in Jewish hands. The present appearance of this name is, as far as I can determine, its first occurrence in any published Mandaean material. One possible exception to this statement seems to be in a Mandaean Diwan edited by J. Euting in 1904 (*Mandaeischer Diwan*, Strassburg). This is illustrated with a number of drawings, and one of these (figure 43) is described in the Latin notes as "Michael Arcangelus." Unfortunately the Mandaean words describing figure 43 are too faint in the facsimile to permit their being read properly, but as far as I can make out, there is no trace of the word Michael.

Ziel (ZY'YL): this reading is being adopted, though there is some support for ZY'WL; its connection with ZYWY'YL in l. 12 is uncertain. Possibly ZY and ZYWY are related to ZYW' ("splendour"). The name Ziel seems to be found nowhere else, although the phrase "the angels of the splendour" is in the Ginza (e.g., G, p. 11, l. 4).

Nadriel (NDRY'YL) may be compared with NYDR'L in Wohlstein's Aram. bowl 2416 (cited in the note on Metatron in l. 6 above), and with

N'ṬR'YL, found at least once in the Ginza (G, p. 168, l. 8; cf. MD, p. 283).

Yhadiel (YHDY'YL): cf. Yhaziel in Text E, l. 8. This name may reflect Jewish influence: YHDY'L appears in B.Heb. (I Chr. 5:24), and Schwab gives YHDY'L as a Jewish name of the zodiacal sign of the Virgin (S, p. 253).

You shall destroy (TYBṬLWN): the 2nd per. pl. imp. Pa.

MYDYM ("anything"): this orthography, which is close to J.Aram. and Syr., is anomalous: the correct Mandaic is MYND'M (MG, p. 186).

Hateful (S'YN'): see the note on this word in Text C, l. 17.

Buktuya: a small defect in the bowl accounts for the mark on the photograph, just below the last letter of this word.

11. *Dwelling* (MDWRT'): this word is well established in Mand. (MD, p. 258). But the house has just been mentioned in the text, and unless there is a distinction between two separate buildings, a second reference to the home seems redundant, although such redundancy appears above in ll. 2–3. I have therefore wondered if we have here the J.Aram. MDWRT' ("wood-pile"). Modern Mandaeans distinguish between clean and unclean wood,[7] and if this distinction was endorsed by the bowl-writer, it would explain the effort to keep the wood-pile free from harm.

WDZ'DWY' occurs twice in this line, and it illustrates the convention of writing the relative pronoun as the letter D when B, W, or L comes immediately before it (MG, p. 92). This suggests that the relative and D were pronounced alike (cf. the note on Duktana Prauk in Text C, l. 9).

Flesh and blood seems here to be equivalent to "people." It is a phrase found in the Ginza, where it refers to the mortal nature of man (G, p. 193, ll. 27–28; cf. MD, p. 62, under *bisra*). For its appearance in a modern Mandaean phylactery, see MP, p. 40, l. 13.

12–13. A number of words in these lines present difficulties for which I am unable to offer solutions. In some cases the correct reading or the proper word division is in doubt, while in others a satisfactory meaning cannot be established.

12. *Adrban* ('DRB'N) occurs three times in this line, though the reading in the third case is uncertain. Presumably it is the name of an angel or spirit, but I can find no reference to it elsewhere. R. A. Bowman has suggested privately that it may be a cryptic form of 'DN RB'N, "the Great Lord"; such words might come easily from a Jewish writer, but this

[7]MII, pp. 109, 137.

is not a Mandaean phrase, nor is ʾDN a common noun in Mand. (cf. Mand. ʾDWNʾY, a name given to the sun, and often used in incantations, MD, p. 7).

Aruhun (ʾRWHWN): this is the most likely reading of an uncertain text. It may be another name of Adrban; possibly it is a corruption of Arhum (ʾRHWM), one of the keepers of a *maṭarta* (G, p. 598).

Amen: Montgomery, in discussing the use of Amen, Selah, Halleluia, etc., in Aramaic incantations, said: "These Jewish terms are not found in the Mandaic texts" (AIT, p. 63). We now know, however, that this is not the case, and that these words are familiar to Mandaean exorcists (AMMB, text M, l. 25; MII, p. 27; MD, p. 22). The conventional rendering "Amen" is retained here, although a close adherence to the Mand. favours "Amin."

Moses of the myriads (MŠH RBWTʾ): this phrase appears to reflect some Jewish influence: the Mand. for Moses is MYŠʾ (cf. B.Heb. MŠH); "myriad" (RWBʾN) is uninflected in Mand. (MG, p. 190), and our text RBWTʾ is very close to the pl. of this word in J.Aram (RBWWTʾ, J, p. 1439). On the place of Moses in incantations, see AIT, pp. 46–47, 107.[8]

I myself am Moses: it is not clear whether the black circle, preceding these words, is a punctuation mark or a smudged letter. I take it that the bowl-writer is here impersonating Moses; cf. the Greek magical phrase, "I am Moses."[9]

KMʾ Ḏ: "just as much as" (cf. MD, p. 218).

Hiel (HYʾYL): cf. the angel HYʾL in S, p. 223, and ḤYʾL, a name in B.Heb. (I Kings 16:34). Possibly, however, from the context and in line with the formation of the next two names, we should assume that our text is in error and that it is meant for Hailel (HYLʾYL), an angel who appears in the Ginza (G, p. 173, l. 27).

Ziwiel: see the note on Ziel in l. 10 above.

Hadriel . . . Hasdiel appear as angels in certain Aramaic texts (AIT, p. 270), and they are also listed in S, pp. 221, 242, but they have hitherto not been found in Mandaean texts. The verb HSD I does not appear in Mand. at all (cf. HSD II, MD, p. 151); *hizda* ("mercy"), recorded in MD, p. 142, is the Mand. cognate to J.Aram. ḤSDʾ.

13. *HWS PS GʾS*: rather than take these words as sheer nonsense, I assume that we have three imperatives, with correct spelling sacrificed to

[8]For various references to Moses in Greek magical papyri, see the index (p. 187) to C. Wessely, "Griechische Zauberpapyrus von Paris und London," in *Denkschriften der kaiserlichen Akademie der Wissenschaften*, Wien, vol. 36 (1888), 2. Abt., pp. 27–208.

[9]Found in Wessely, *ibid.*, p. 129, l. 109.

the whim of the exorcist. HWS, from HWŠ ("hasten"), the latter meaning not being given in MD, p. 138; PS, from PSS ("vanish"); G'S from KSS I ("crumble," "perish"), as in MD, p. 221; on G and K in Mand. see MG, p. 40.

The great Qmiel (QMY'YYL): cf. the human name QMW'L in B.Heb. (Gen. 22:21). Schwab gives Qmiel as the name of an angel (S, p. 350), but this is its first appearance in a Mandaean source. Against taking the text to be "before the great El" is the fact that while QMY is good J.Aram., the only Mand. forms of this preposition are Q'M and 'Q'M (MG, p. 194). The great El is a being mentioned in the Ginza in connection with Ruha (G, p. 260, l. 20).

Antun ('NTWN) occurs twice in this line, but the meaning is obscure in both cases, partly because of four troublesome words which I have left untranslated. It can hardly be the personal pronoun ("you" pl.), for this appears in its normal form ('N'TWN) in ll. 9, 10. Possibly it is a form of Anatan ('N'T'N), who appears in the Ginza (G, p. 598) as well as in S, p. 178; however, in Mandaean thought this being is malevolent (MD, p. 24).

'YYR is an uncertain reading; it may represent 'Y'R, "ether."

Ḏ Y'B'̱ seems to be the correct reading, but I can extract no meaning from it. The ending '̱ suggests that we have a common noun rather than a p.n.

Seven upper firmaments: the text is legible except for "firmaments," of which only the first two letters are certain. On "firmament" see the note in Text C, l. 8. Ordinarily Mandaeanism recognizes only one firmament, although in the Ginza there are references to a plurality of firmaments (e.g., G, p. 199, l. 3). One text in the Drower collection has the phrase "the seven firmaments" (MD, p. 437), and in the Ginza reference just given the firmaments are associated with seven water-mists. I note one passage in the Qulasta which alludes to the seven sides of the firmament (Q, p. 9, l. 8). Possibly there is a connection between the phrase in our text and the seven heavens of Judaism.

Priel (PRY'YL): this word appears in one of Lidzbarski's bowls, but the bracket after the first letter indicates some textual uncertainty (MZ, text 3). Probably this name is to be identified with PR'YL, PRW'YL, P'R'YL (MD, p. 380) found in various Mandaean texts (MZ, text 1 a,c; IMCK, p. 97; AMMB, text M; cf. PRYL in Text E of this study, l. 17). Both Montgomery and Gordon take this name to be a form of Raphael (AIT, p. 272; AMMB, p. 99).

LYBṬWLYN is being taken as the imp. Pa. ("let them destroy"), although the correct orthography for this is LYB'ṬLWN.

*MYN*ʾ *D̲* must be either "from the person of" or "from the property of."

14. *Satans* (STʾNYʾ) are a subclass of evil spirits (as in AIT, bowl 35, l. 3) who appear in the Ginza (e.g., G, p. 39, l. 28); the s. form can have the meaning Satan (e.g., G, p. 16, l. 15; cf. MD, p. 311). It is probable that this word entered Mandaean thought from some Jewish source: it appears in Jewish literature in the pl. with the sense of evil beings as early as the book of Enoch (40:7; 65:6).

Threshold (ʾSQWPTʾ): this orthography is closer to J.Aram. than to normal Mand.; cf. the note on this word in Text C, l. 23.

14–15. *And from their sons* (WMN BYWN): a defect in the bowl separates the first W from the following MN. BYWN is an error for BNʾYWN (which appears in l. 18).

15. SʾLH: this orthography appears in two Aramaic bowls (AIT, bowl 20, l. 6; bowl 24, ll. 3, 6); the usual Mand. is SʾLʾ, as later in l. 18 (cf., MD, p. 312). The conventional rendering "Selah" is retained here, although the Mand. favours "Sala(h)." It is one of the curiosities of magic that this somewhat obscure biblical word (probably a musical direction and found almost exclusively in the Psalms) came in the course of time to have magical value.

At this point in the text there appear the following magic signs:

h g f e d c b a

k j i

r q q p o n m l

s t s

The groups of letters of the alphabet call for no comment; alphabetic nonsense was standard incantation practice and was seemingly at the caprice of the bowl-writer. Brief notes are offered on the non-alphabetic signs. While the author-artist may have felt free to improvise symbols of his own, it is likely that he drew largely from the traditional stock-in-trade, of whose origin and history he was perhaps quite unaware.

a. Unless this is a variant of the cross motif (see *q* below), this may be a monogram made up of the letters W and Z.

b. This may be an echo of an Egyptian hieroglyph, possibly either "hoe" or "hobble for cattle." Or it may be the Mandaean version of a sign which appears on the Pergamon divining disk of the third century A.D., reproduced in AS, p. 458.

c. This may be a conventionalized Magic Hand (on the hand in magic, see AS, pp. 467f.). I note that there is a superficial resemblance between our sign and the Egyptian hieroglyph for "plants growing in a pot": the latter has strokes issuing from the top of the pot.

d. I can find no parallel to this.

e. This appears twice, with other magic symbols, in a fourth or fifth century Greek papyrus edited by F. G. Kenyon.[10] A somewhat similar sign, but upside-down, appears in a Syriac text published by Gordon (IES, l. 16).

f. I can find no parallel to this.

g. This may be a variant of *a* above.

h. This may be the Greek Epsilon, put in because of its resemblance to the crescent moon, or it may be intended for the Delphic Epsilon.[11]

i. A symbol very similar to this appears twice on the disk referred to in *b* above.

j. I can find no parallel to this.

k. This may be a glorified form of the letter G. It may, however, be the Mandaean form of a similar sign (but facing in the opposite direction) found three times on the disk referred to in *b* above.

l. This may represent the Evil Eye, or it may be a sign for the sun or for sunshine. A close parallel appears in figure 91 of F. Lexa, *La Magie dans l'Egypte antique*, vol. 3 (Paris, 1925); another parallel, but with the strokes at the right of the circle, is found on a Coptic amulet in figure 159. There is also an Azilian pictograph of western Europe, consisting of two circles side by side, each with downward strokes, given on p. 16 of D. A. Mackenzie, *The Migration of Symbols* (London and New York, 1926).

m. This is likely a foot or boot, perhaps to convey the idea that the

[10] *Greek Papyri in the British Museum: Catalogue with Texts*, 1893, Papyrus CXXIV, p. 121; plate 69, folio of facsimiles.

[11] C. W. King, *The Gnostics and Their Remains*, 2nd ed. (London, 1887), p. 297.

evil spirits are being kicked away; there are Hittite and Egyptian hieroglyphs that are rather similar to it. Other parallels occur on the disk mentioned in *b* above, and still another among the symbols in the Greek papyrus mentioned in *e* above.

n. The only parallel I can find for this, but in a horizontal position, is in Lexa, *La Magie* . . ., vol. 3, figure 91.

o. This may represent a serpent about to strike its victim, or it may be a symbol of the Gnostic Chnoubis, sometimes regarded as a god of healing (AS, p. 205). A somewhat similar, though more angular sign appears three times on the Pergamon disk (see *b* above). A closer parallel, looking like the Coptic letter Xi, is found with other signs in a Greek papyrus edited by Wessely.[12] Our sign also resembles the Kabbalistic symbol for the spirit of Jupiter (AS, p. 391).

p. A single stroke topped by a circle occurs as a mason's mark in Egypt.[13] It appears also on an Akkadian seal.[14] In both these instances this sign may be a conventionalized sacred tree, or the sun disk on a standard. It also appears, in a slanting or horizontal position, with other magic symbols in a third century Greek papyrus edited by F. G. Kenyon,[15] and in another Greek papyrus edited by C. Wessely.[16]

q. The cross is termed by Budge "one of the oldest amuletic signs in the world" (AS, p. 336). It appears once on the Pergamon disk (see *b* above); in Lexa, *La Magie* . . ., vol. 3, figure 88; and twice in the Syr. text published by Gordon (IES, ll. 1, 14b).

r. This may be an unusual form of the Mand. D or R. Or it may be the same symbol that appears in Lexa, *op. cit.*, figure 91. Or it may be an echo of the Egyptian hieroglyph for "gazelle's rib."

s. See the note on *l* above. Signs identical with, or similar to it have a widespread dissemination. I cite the following examples: on an Azilian pictograph in D. A. Mackenzie (*The Migration of Symbols*, p. 16); on belemnites recorded by S. Seligmann;[17] on stone vases and on bathroom decoration in western Asia;[18] on a Coptic amulet in Lexa (*La Magie* . . ., vol. 3, figure 158).

t. It seems improbable that this is a variation upon the foregoing (*s*).

[12]Wessely, "Griechische Zauberpapyrus . . .," p. 112.

[13]*Medinet Habu Graffiti*, ed. by W. F. Edgerton (Chicago, 1937), plate 89.

[14]*Ancient Oriental Seals in the Collection of Mr. Edward T. Newell*, ed. by H. H. von der Osten (Chicago, 1934), seal 288.

[15]Kenyon, *Greek Papyri in the British Museum* . . ., Papyrus CXXI, plates 53, 63.

[16]Wessely, "Griechische Zauberpapyrus . . .," p. 55.

[17]*Die magischen Heil- und Schutzmittel aus der unbelebten Natur* (Stuttgart, 1927), figures 52, 53.

[18]M. Pezard, *Mission à Bender-Bouchir* (Paris, 1914), plate VIII; G. Loud, *Khorsabad*, part I (Chicago, 1936), plate I.

A very similar sign, but with the lower horizontal stroke missing, is found with other magic symbols in a papyrus edited by Kenyon.[19] In view of the magical use of names, one cannot but wonder whether this sign is related to the square with a dot in its centre, which appears in the Greek magical papyri as a symbol or abbreviation for "name" or "names."[20]

15. *Spells of all . . . spirits*: this phrase may refer to the preceding array of magic signs. For an attributive adjective in the emphatic state, with a noun in the absolute, see MG, p. 317. The use of RWHYN to denote a species of evil spirits is common in J.Aram. and Syr.; it is also familiar in Mandaean writings (e.g., G, p. 54, l. 1; Q, p. 24, l. 6). On the various meanings of RWH' in Mand., see MD, p. 428.

16. *Male and female Liliths*: on Liliths, see the note in l. 8 of this text. The Lilith is normally a female being and her male counterpart is the Lili (as in AMMB, text K; cf. AE, l. 7). Our present phrase is therefore somewhat unusual, although it is found in one of Lidzbarski's texts (MZ, bowl V). I note that in one of Gordon's bowls we have "lilis, male and female" (AMB, text A, l. 3).

I have bound . . . sealed: on this use of the p. part., see MG, p. 381.

Unbreakable: I am taking MYŠTRY' as the Etta. part. absolute pl. (MG, pp. 164, 265).

MWMY': as the context does not favour taking this as the pl. of "spot," "blemish," I suggest that this is the pl. of MWM' II (from YM'), that it means "exorcism" (cf. MWMY in J.Aram., Jast., p. 743), and that it is the m. form of the Mand. *mumata* (MD, p. 262).

'N' 'H W' DYKRT' MWY'YN 'N'T': these words, at first glance, seem to make no sense, and they may as such constitute the exorcisms just mentioned. But, modifying a proposal made privately by R. A. Bowman, I suggest that this is a somewhat garbled J.Aram. sentence with the force of a spell: "I am a kinsman, and I will invoke (W'DYKR) a decree (taking T'M to be Ṭ'M), and it will guard (WY'YN, Pa. of 'WN) the (household) vessels ('N'T'; see AIT, bowl 38, l. 3, a Mand. text)."

Akmahin . . . Cain: either these two persons are to serve as scapegoats upon whom the evil spirits, who have been annoying Buktuya and his family, are to settle, or these individuals are for some reason being brought under the protection of the bowl.

Akmahin ('KM'HYN), I assume, is the name of a person, although I have not found it elsewhere. It may be related to the Syr. KMH', "blind" (with a cognate in Arabic).

[19]Kenyon, *Greek Papyri in the British Museum . . .*, Papyrus CXXI, plate 63.
[20]Kenyon, *ibid.*, p. 251; Wessely, "Griechische Zauberpapyrus . . .," p. 43.

BYŠ': in view of the subsequent "leprous," I am taking this as "sickly," a meaning which it sometimes has in J.Aram. (Jast., p. 167).

Cain (Q'Y'N): I take this to be the Mand. form of the B.Heb. QYN, which may have come into Mand. from either Jewish or Christian sources (cf. Syr. Q'YN), though a Persian or Arabic source cannot be ruled out.[21]

GRB'N'; the usual form of this word in Mand. is GYRB'N' (MD, p. 92).

17. *Comrades in the night and for companionship in the day*: I assume that these words are in apposition to the preceding phrase ("Buktuya . . . Shirin"). "For companionship" (L'Ṣ'WT') seems a rather unexpected counterpart to "comrades" (HBRY'), but I can make nothing else out of the text. YMM' is found in J.Aram. (Jast., p. 580), and it appears as 'YM'M' in a Mandaean text in AIT (bowl 39, l. 10), but the latter word is not recorded in MD. Our present text has an interesting parallel in one of Gordon's Aramaic bowls, L' HBR' BYMM' WL' ṢWT' BLYLYH, which is rendered "no company by day and no society by night" (AMMB, text K, pp. 92–93, and Addenda on p. 106). This translation seems to make little sense in its context, and I suspect that our present text supplies the clue to the understanding of Gordon's Aramaic.

The following symbols appear in the text at this point:

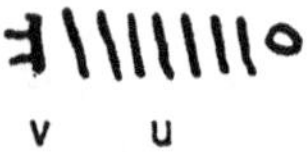

u. This is presumably the letter Z written seven times. Undoubtedly the seventh letter of the alphabet written seven times would have some special significance. In one of Montgomery's Aramaic bowls seven Alephs and seven crosses are used (AIT, bowl 31, l. 8), and in Text B of this study seven Waws in l. 6 appear to have magical force.

v. I can find no parallel to this.

17. *'L 'Z' HL' NZQM*: I take it that this is a magic phrase. As it seems impossible to make sense of it as Mand., I suggest, following a lead from R. A. Bowman, that it is a Jewish spell, or the beginning of one, and that it may be rendered: "Against the Strong One are there not injuries?" I note that Schwab lists 'Z' as a fallen Jewish angel (S, p. 321, although his reference to the book of Enoch seems to be erroneous), and that in the Mandaean Qulasta 'Z RB' ("the great Az") occurs as the name of a spirit (Q, p. 22, l. 5; in Drower's version of this in CPM, p. 11, l. 7, it is wrongly rendered as "the Great BAZ"). I observe that in three of Montgomery's bowls (AIT, bowl 21, l. 2; bowl 22, l. 2; bowl 23, l. 2) NZQ occurs in the pl., being rendered as "injurers."

[21] Cf. S. Haïm, *Persian-English Dictionary* (Teheran, 1953), p. 621.

18. After "all the threshold of" and after "all the people" there are chips at the edge of the bowl, but the lacunae caused thereby can be readily filled in.

ZYKY' is an error for ZYKRY'.

Yea ('YYN) is given in MD both as 'YN (p. 15) and as ʿYN (p. 348). It seems to be rare in incantations: I have noticed it in only one other Mandaean bowl, where it appears in the same phrase as in the present text (IMCK, bowl 13, last line; pp. 14 (note 2), 37–41).

Finished (ŠLYM') is doubtless equivalent to *finis*. I have not noticed any other magic text concluding in this way.

BOWL E (949.94)

Introduction

TEXT E is on an unevenly made, wide, open bowl (height, 5.3 cm.; diameter at top, 17.7 cm.; diameter at base, 4 cm.; thickness, 0.5 cm.) of unknown provenance. The spiral inscription in Mandaic requires eighteen lines in the interior of the bowl, and on the whole it is reasonably legible, although there are four places, as indicated in the transcription, where it is impossible to make out what is written. The ideology and vocabulary of the inscription are clearly Mandaean.

The incantation is designed to protect Anush Busai, son of Narsai Dukt, his wife, children, and property, from various evils. The allusions to these real or potential troubles are too vague to permit the identification of the family situation that called for the writing of this spell. It may have been merely the building of a new house.

Text

(1) בשומ̣איון ד̱ חייא וזרזתא וחתמתא (2) ונטרתא
תחוילא לביתא דורא̱ היכלא̱ ובניאנא̱ (3) אנוש
בוסאי ב̣ר נארסאי דוכת גב.א ... כעויא (4) פת
אנושתאי ואסותא תחוי לשירזאד ולקישאגי. בחאר
בניא (5) מוש̣כריא ולאברון ולאמחו ... ...
אתון וקניאנון זׄיד זרארא ד̱ ראזיא על (6)
שומיא ועל ארקא עתקריא כיבשא ... על שומיא

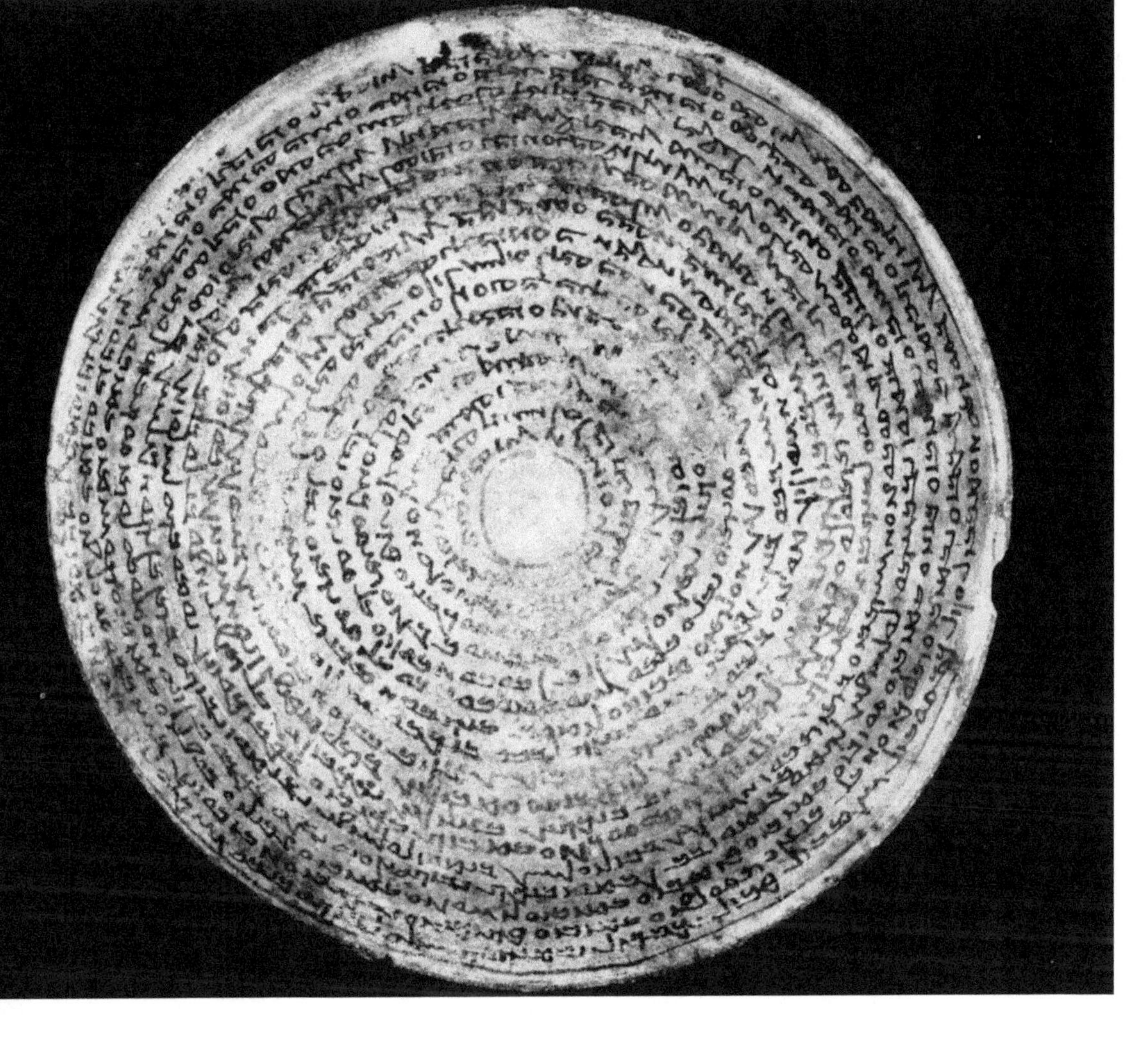

ועל ארקא חוא אסארא רבא על (7) שומיא ועל
ארקא קריויא ליאואר עותרא מזרזא מנחראנון ד
אלמיא קריויא ליאואר עותרא ד קדום (8)
חות..ל לאלמא קום אזיל חוזיא למאדא ד ראבותא
ד חו ברא בות נפשא חא יחזיעל ברא בוכרא
חוזיא (9) ... ד קרא חזאנון לשובעא ותריסאר
ד בנא ד חאסירתא ד חאיזין סאגיא בלבאב שומיא
זארינון בזיר ראזא ד (10) רישאיון בחאנון
נתכביש כבושינון בכיבשא רבא ד בחימיאן
חדאריא נתכובשון ד רישאיון לתכביש אסרינון
במאספוסיתא (11) ד חאוינון ראזאיון ד על
בורכאיון לאברכון חבאלון אכסתא ד לא
לחיוילון ממלאלא אפוכונון לממלאלון על
דוכתון רגולינון ופכרינון על (12) מנטול
ד טאבו לאבאדאנא במא ד מפסדנא בליא בגו
בורא סחית וחבית כיבשא לעותריא ועסרית
חילאיון ד מאשכניא עסרית עכוריא בפריכאיון
(13) ואקארתא לחילאיון מינאיון ואסרתינון
לשידיא ודיויא ובאסילתינון מן אלמא חאשכית
שראגיא ד חומריא במימראי ד חינון בדיליא
לחון בוסאי לא לחיטו ובוסאי וביתא (14)
במזרזותא ד כולחון בישיא מינא לדחלון
נתיסרון ונצטמרון סחריא ודיויא בדיליא
בוסאי וברחמאי לאלחיטון לתסאר בוסאי בר
נרסאי דוכת וביתא וזאוא ובנא בכבאר זיוא
(15) ד אסארא לא מישתריא לא מישתריא אסארא
וחאתמא לא מיתיברון מנטול ד עסיריא סחריא
ועסיריא דיויא עסיריא שידיא עסיריא פיקדיא
עסיריא ליחאביא עסיריא גדוליא באטליא (16)
עסיריא מאחיקיא עסירא חומריא עסירא רוחיא

עסיריא דמו דמו עסיריא שובעא עסיריא
תריסאר כוכביא ועסיריא מלאכיא ד על רוגזא
משלסיא עסיריא פתיכריא ועכוריא ד עידאיון
בחירבא (17) שאליסיא עסירא עידאיון
עסיריא תביריא גנפאיון תביריא רישאיון
ושאקאיון ושדקתינון בשומא ד אסרעיל אזיל
כבשעיל חנקעיל פריל וכרכיל ועסותא
תחוילא לביתא דורא חיכלא ובניאנא
(18) ד בוסאי בר נרסאידוכת וחייא זאכין

Translation

(1) In the name of Life! And may there be girding and sealing (2) and safeguard to the house, the dwelling, the habitation, and the building (3) of Anush Busai, son of Narsai Dukt . . . . K'wya, (4) daughter of Anushtai; and may there be healing to Shirzad and to Qishagi Bhar, his sons, (5) the musk-coloured ones; and let them remove and let them smite (?) . . . . and their property; provided is the protection (knot?) of the secret spells against (6) the heaven and against the earth; the exorcism shall be invoked . . . . against the heaven and against the earth; the great spell is against (7) the heaven and against the earth; invocations to Yawar Uthra who girds the illuminators of the worlds; invocations to Yawar Uthra who is before (8) Hathmel(?) for ever; arise, go, behold the Lord of Greatness who created the prayer of the soul; lo, Yhaziel his first-born son; behold (9) . . . . whom he called; see (them) the Seven and the Twelve who are the sons of the Faulty One whom many see; in the heart of heaven they scatter them (they are scattered?); dispersed is the secret (secret plan?) of (10) their heads in their privy parts; their dominions (exorcisms?) shall be pressed down with the great exorcism which is in the glorious girdle; they shall be pressed down so that their heads will be pressed; bind them with the fetters (11) which revealed their secrets so that upon their knees they will kneel down; may fury be their ruin; so that they will be speechless; pervert their speech; in their place hobble them and tie them (12) for the sake of goodness to destruction, according to what (just as?) I destroy what is decayed in the midst of the fire; I have cleansed and I have hidden the exorcism for the *uthras*, and I have bound the powers of the cult-huts. I have bound the temple-demons

in their (pagan) shrines, (13) and I have unrooted (it) their powers from them, and I have bound the devils and the demons, and I have destroyed them from the world. I have darkened the lamps of the amulet-spirits by my words, so that they because of them may not entangle Busai. And Busai and his house are (14) under protection so that all the evil ones shall be afraid of him. The sorcery-spirits and the demons shall be bound and pressed down for the sake of Busai, and because of my prayers they will not entangle, you will not bind, Busai, son of Narsai Dukt, or his house or his wife or his sons; by Kbar-Ziwa (15) which is a spell not to be loosened, not to be loosened; the spell and the seal are unbreakable because the sorcery-spirits are bound and the demons are bound; the devils are bound; the demon-visitants are bound; the net-spirits are bound; the useless hairy ones are bound; (16) the tormentors are bound; the amulet-spirits are bound; the spirits are bound; all kinds of effigies are bound; the Seven are bound; the twelve stars are bound; and the (evil) angels who are appointed over anger are bound; the idol-demons and the temple-demons who are the rulers over their festivals with a sword (or "with destruction") are bound; (17) their festivals are bound; their arms are bound, broken; their heads and their legs are broken; and I have silenced them in the name of Asrel, Azel, Kabshiel, Hnaqel, Prel, and Krakel; and may healing be to the house, the dwelling, the habitation, and the building (18) of Busai, son of Narsai Dukt; and Life is victorious!

Commentary

1–2. For the vocabulary, see notes on Text C, l. 15, and Text D, ll. 1–3.

3. *Anush* ('NWŠ): this may go back to the well-known Semitic root 'NŠ, but as many Mandaean personal names are of Persian vintage, it is tempting to assume that it came into Mand. from some Persian source. In any case it serves as a common name in Pers. (Justi, pp. 17–18, 484). Whatever its origin, it is the name of an important Mandaean *uthra* (MD, p. 26; on *uthra*, see the note on Zhir in Text C, l. 14), and it is also a name given to people. In the latter sense it occurs in Pognon's bowls, but the sex of the person is uncertain (IMCK, bowls 16 and 24); in one bowl (IMCK, bowl 21) it is clearly part of a woman's name.

Busai (BWS'Y): I can find no other instance of this proper name. It does not appear among Justi's Pers. names, except that *būs* is recorded as the second element in one name, Aškebūs (Justi, p. 490). If it is of Persian origin, it must be from *būs* ("a kiss"), which is also found in Arabic.

Narsai Dukt: cf. the Persian name Narsidukhte (Justi, p. 226).

Narsai (N'RS'Y): for *narseh* in Persian names, see Justi, pp. 225, 504 (cf. Pers. *nars*, "unripe," "green").

Dukt (DWKT): see the note on Duktan in Text C, l. 2.

K'wya (K'WY'): for Kahweh, Kawi, Qawiya as Persian names, see Justi, pp. 160, 499.

4. *Anushtai* ('NWŠT'Y) is presumably the same name that occurs as 'NWŠT' (a woman) in IMCK, bowl 14, l. 1.

Shirzad (ŠYRZ'D) is a Persian name (Justi, p. 298); both elements of it (*šir* and *zad*) are common in Persian names (Justi, pp. 294–298, 377, 519).

Qishagi (QYŠ'GY): the reading of Q and G is uncertain. Such a name does not appear elsewhere (cf. Pers. *qīš*, "(woman's) hair"). I note that in Justi, Kasagos is recorded in Greek (p. 158).

Bhar (BH'R) must be related to the Persian name Behar recorded in Justi, p. 66; it is also the second element in another Persian name (Justi, p. 487). In Mand. the word occurs as a common noun meaning "spring" (MD, p. 53); it is also part of a woman's name, Bhar'zag (MD, p. 54). In all these cases it goes back to the Pers. *bhār*, "spring."

5. *Musk-coloured* (MWŠKWY'): it is improbable that this is an ethnic or geographical term; cf. Syr. MWŠKY', "*Moschi*, a race between the Black and Caspian Seas."[1] It is more likely a common adjective descriptive of the sons, and comes from Pers. *mšky*, "musk-coloured," from *mšk*, "musk"; cf. the Persian names Muškī, Muškōi, Muškūyeh, cited by Justi, p. 218.

Let them remove (L'BRWN) is the 3rd m. pl. imp. Aph. of BR' (MD, p. 69). It is a feature of this text that the preformative L is generally used in the 3rd per. imp. rather than N (cf. MG, pp. 215–16).

Let them smite (?) (L'MHW): presumably a final N is missing, if this is the Aph. of MH' ("strike," etc.). This verb, however, is not used in the Aph. in Mand. or in J.Aram., and in Syr. the Aph. is uncommon.

Provided (ZYD): MD (p. 164) supports this as the Pe. p. part., although in J. Aram. and Syr. this verb is commonly used in the Pa.

Protection (*knot?*) (ZR'R'): MD, which gives three references to this word in magical texts (p. 85, under *gupta*; p. 170), takes this as a variant (originally a miscopying?) of *zrada*, "casing," for which Syr. ZRD', "coat of mail," is cited (the latter also appears in J.Aram., Jast.,

[1] J. P. Margoliouth, *Supplement to the Thesaurus Syriacus of R. Payne Smith* (Oxford, 1927), p. 189.

p. 411). It is tempting to look for some other explanation of this word: possibly it is from J.Aram. ZWR, which in the Pa. means "tie up" (cf. Syr. ṢRR', "knot," from ṢR; Mand. ṢRR II, "tie up," which gives us Ṣ'R'RT', "bag," MD, p. 388).

Secret spells is apparently the meaning of R'ZY', as in Text C, ll. 3, 16, 20.

6. *Heaven . . . earth*: for a somewhat similar use of these words, cf. IMCK, bowl 13, pp. 36–37.

HW' appears to be the perf. of "to be," which is sometimes used as a present tense (MD, p. 133).

7. *Invocations* (QRYWY'), which appears twice in this line, is presumably the pl. of QRYW', which does not appear in MD, in J.Aram., or in Syr. It must either be "invocations" or have the same meaning as Mand. *QYRY'T'* 2, "incantations" (MD, p. 412).

Yawar (Y'W'R) is an outstanding *uthra* (MD, p. 185; CPM, p. 252, note 2).

Girds (MZRZ') is the a. part. Pa. of ZRZ.

Illuminators (MNHR'NWN): cf. MD, p. 248; probably the sun and moon are meant (cf. G, p. 25, l. 3).

QDWM is probably an error for QWDM ("before"); see note on QDYM in Text D, l. 6.

8. *HWT . . . L* may be H'TM'YL an angel who appears in the Ginza (G, p. 168, l. 8) and elsewhere (MD, p. 128).

For ever (L'LM'): MD, p. 20, cites this expression in the form *lalam.*

HWZY' (twice in this line) is the imv. of HZ' with 3rd m. s. suffix (MG, p. 287; MD, p. 138).

Lord of Greatness is one of the names for the Supreme Being in Mandaeanism (e.g., G., p. 6, l. 8; p. 7, ll. 13–14; etc.; CPM, p. 2, ll. 2–3; etc.).

BWT ("prayer") is the Mand. cognate to J.Aram. B'WT'.

H' ("lo") is the interjection recorded in MD, p. 115.

Yhaziel (YHZY'L): the text is slightly doubtful. I can find no other reference to this angel, which is strange in view of his alleged relation to the Lord of Greatness (cf. Y'HŠY'YL in MD, p. 185, also the name in B.Heb. Jahaziel (YHZY'L) in I Chr. 12:4). Yhadiel appears as an angel in Text D, l. 10.

9. *HZ'NWN*: I assume this to be an error for HZYNWN ("see them").

ŠWBʿʾ: this occurs again in l. 16. It is a J.Aram. form for "seven"; the normal Mand. forms are ŠWBʾ, ŠʾBʾ (MG, p. 188; MD, p. 452).

The Seven and the Twelve are the seven planets and the twelve signs of the Zodiac (as later in l. 16 of this text); the combination occurs in G, p. 24, l. 27; p. 143, l. 3; p. 330, ll. 2–3; CPM, p. 98, l. 7; p. 144, ll. 31–32. In the Mandaean daily baptism, called *rishama*, the Seven and the Twelve are repudiated in the last act of the ceremony.[2] On the planets as the creation of Ruha, see note on "the five angels of this world" in Text C, l. 6. The Twelve were also the offspring of Ruha (MII, p. 256).

The Faulty One (HʾSYRTʾ): see MD, p. 125. Ruha is thus described in TTQ, p. 200, l. 12.

BNʾ is either an error for BNYʾ, or we have, as in l. 14, the 3rd s. suffix, giving us "his (or 'her') sons" (MG, p. 178).

HʾYZYN is presumably the a. part. pl., which should be HʾZYN.

The heart of heaven occurs in the Ginza; see MD, p. 228, under *lbab.*

ZʾRYNWN: while this word is hardly legible, I am taking it as the Pe. a. part. pl., with suffix, of ZRʾ, "scatter."

BZYR is the Pe. p. part. of BZR, "disperse," "strew," which is found in B. Heb. and J. Aram. This root is presumably a variant of the Mand. BDR (MD, p. 52).

10. *Their dominions* (KBWŠYNWN): probably this is the J.Aram. KYBWŠ, "conquest," "dominion" (Jast., p. 630); otherwise it must be a variant or a misspelling of Mand. KYBŠʾ, "mastery," "exorcism," the next word in this line.

The great exorcism (KYBŠʾ RBʾ): this phrase, translated "master-spell," is quoted in MD, p. 212.

Girdle (HYMYʾN) is an important part of the ritual dress of the Mandeans.[3] It is not clear whether the present text refers to the power inherent in this ritual girdle, or whether the reference is metaphorical; cf. this passage from the Ginza: "Bindet euch Gürtel um die Hüften gleich den Gürteln des Glanzes, die die Uthras des Lichtes sich um die Hüften binden" (G, p. 44, ll. 33–35; cf. p. 589, l. 28).

HDʾRYʾ ("glories"): in MD the s. of this word is given as *hadra* (p. 116), or *hidra* (p. 141).

ʾSRYNWN is the Pe. imv., with 3rd pl. suffix (MD, p. 29).

11. *They will kneel down* (LʾBRKWN) is the Aph. imp. of BRK.

Fury (ʾKSTʾ) is a common noun (MD, p. 16), but it is not clear whose fury is meant.

[2]MII, p. 104. [3]MII, p. 31.

LHYWYLWN is an error for LYHWYLWN.

ʾPWKWNWN is the Pe. imv. of ʾPK.

RGWLYNWN is the Pe. imv. of RGL.

12. *For the sake of* (MNṬWL): a somewhat commoner orthography for this word is ʾMYNṬWL (MD, p. 22).

Ṭʾ BW seems here to mean "goodness." This word is, however, also used to designate a ritual meal (MD, p. 172; MII, p. 140).

Destruction (ʾBʾDʾNʾ): this orthography is close to that of the cognate in B.Heb. The usual Mand. is ʾBDʾNʾ (MD, p. 3).

According to what (BMʾ D̲): cf. MD, p. 237.

I destroy (MPSDNʾ): this is a defective orthography of the Aph. a. part. of PSD with suffix. MD (p. 375), which records this verb, but not in the Aph., cites the Arabic cognate but not the J.Aram. (Jast., p. 1192).

What is decayed (BLYʾ): while the reading is uncertain, it is being taken as the p. part. Pe. of BLʾ II, "be worn out," "decay" (MD, p. 65).

I have cleansed (SHYT): this verb is not cited in MD, but it appears both in Syr. and in J.Aram. In the latter cognates the transitive, "wash (something)," is a meaning found only in the Pa. and Aph. Here the reference may be to a particular act in the praxis of bowl magic.

Exorcism (KYBŠʾ) as in l. 10. Here the reference may be to the bowl on which the spell is written.

Uthras: see note on Zhir in Text C, l. 14. As *uthras* are benevolent, the meaning here must be that the *uthras* are called upon for assistance and protection.

Powers: the reference may be to evil spirits troubling the cult-huts.

Cult-huts (MʾŠKNYʾ): every sizable Mandaean community today has its own Manda or cult-hut. This is a small gable-roofed building which is entered only by the priests, never by the laity. It is always located by a river bank, and in its courtyard, which the laity may use, there is a lustration pool.[4]

ʿKWRYʾ (also in l. 16) can mean either pagan temples or temple-demons; probably here it has the latter meaning. For this second meaning the cognates in J.Aram. and Syr. offer a more convincing etymology than that suggested in MD, p. 349.

13. *Amulet-spirits* (HWMRYʾ): the s. of this is HWMʾRTʾ (MD, p. 135).

BDYLYʾ: this word, which occurs again in l. 14, is not mentioned either

[4]Chapter 8 in MII, pp. 124–45.

in MG or in MD. Presumably it is the Mand. form of the J.Aram. BDYL, "on account of," etc. (Jast., p. 140).

LHWN ("them"): the antecedent must be "my words."

They . . . entangle (LHYṬW): cf. LHYṬWN in l. 14. This must be the Pa. imp. of ḤWṬ. MD (p. 135) records only the Pe. of this verb, but J.Aram. and Syr. have the Pa. In J.Aram. the Pa. can mean "fasten," "strap," as well as "sew," whence the rendition "entangle" in our translation.

14. *NṢṬMRWN* is the Etta. of ṢMR II, "press down," etc.

Sorcery-spirits (SHRY'): see the note on this word in Text C, l. 6.

My prayers (RHM'Y): the pl. of R'HM' ("friend," "mercy") can designate the Mandaean ritual prayers.

You will not bind (LTS'R): the negative with 2nd m. s. imp. Pe. of 'SR. The change in person and number seems strange, but I can make nothing else out of the text.

Kbar-Ziwa (KB'R ZYW') is an important Mandaean Being (G, p. 67, ll. 18–20; p. 75, ll. 1–4).

15. *MYTYBRWN*: the Ethpe. part. (MG, p. 230); WN must be careless writing for YN.

15–16. With this assortment of evil spirits, cf. the long description of evil beings assisting Darkness in G, p. 277, ll. 35ff.

15. *Useless hairy ones* (GDWLY' B'ṬLY'): MD renders this phrase as "vain spectres" (under *gdula*, p. 80), and as "illusory phantoms" (under *baṭla*, p. 47). The J.Aram. and Syr. cognates support "hairy ones" as a rendition of GDWLY'.

16. *M'HYQY'*: the Aph. part. of HWQ.

All kinds of effigies (DMW DMW): on this distributive use of the absolute state, see MG, p. 301; MD, p. 111.

Seven . . . twelve: see the note on these words in l. 9 of this text.

Anger (RWGZ'): see the note on "stars of anger" in Text C, l. 18.

Their festivals ('YD'YWN) is found also in l. 17. It is a word not recorded in MD, but it appears to be the J.Aram. 'YD (Jast., p. 1067), "idolatrous festival" (cf. Syr. 'YD', "custom," "habit," often used with an appropriate adjective to denote heathen customs).

HYRB' can mean "sword," "battle," "destruction" (MD, p. 126).

17. *GNP'YWN*: GNP', "wing," seems here to have the meaning "arm" as in G, p. 85, l. 19; cf. MD, p. 77.

I have silenced them (ŠDQTYNWN): this is presumably the Pa. of

ŠDQ (cf. J. Aram. ŠTQ), although MD (p. 450) records only the Pe. of this verb.

Asrel (ʾSRʿYL): cf. ʾSRʿYYL in MD, p. 30.

Azel (ʾZYL): cf. ʾZYʾL in S, p. 161.

Kabshiel (KBŠʿYL) is found twice in IMCK, p. 95; it appears in an Aramaic bowl (AMB, text D, l. 14), and as KBŠYʾL in S, p. 264.

Hnaqel (HNQʿYL) seems to be found nowhere else.

Prel (PRYL): cf. the note on Priel in Text D, l. 13.

Krakel (KRKYL): cf. KRKYʾL in S, p. 269.

Healing (ʿSWTʾ): this is read, doubtfully, in Text C, l. 2; cf. the more normal ʾSWTʾ in Text C, ll. 15, 22; Text D, l. 17; MD, p. 28.

18. *Life is victorious!*: see the note on this phrase in Text C, l. 16.

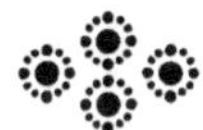

BIBLIOGRAPHY

General, Excluding Magical Texts

Budge, E. A. Wallis

Amulets and Superstitions, London, 1930.

Contenau, G.

La Magie chez les Assyriens et les Babyloniens, Paris, 1947; on magic bowls, see pp. 286–288.

Drower, E. S.

"Mandaean Writings," in *Iraq*, vol. 1 (1934), pp. 171–82.

The Canonical Prayerbook of the Mandaeans, Leiden, 1959.

The Mandaeans of Iraq and Iran, London, 1937; 2nd ed., 1962.

The Thousand and Twelve Questions, Berlin, 1960.

Drower, E. S. and R. Macuch

A Mandaic Dictionary, London, 1963.

Epstein, J. N.

"Gloses babylo-araméennes," in *Revue des études juives*, vol. 73 (1921), pp. 27–58; vol. 74 (1922), pp. 40–72.

Gordon, C. H.

The Living Past, New York, 1941; chapter x is entitled "A World of Demons and Liliths."

Jastrow, M.

A Dictionary of the Targumim, the Talmud Babli and Yerushalmi, and the Midrashic Literature, 2 vols., London, 1903.

Justi, F.

Iranisches Namenbuch, Marburg, 1895.

Lidzbarski, M.

Das Johannesbuch der Mandäer, vol. 1, Text, Giessen, 1905; vol. 2, Einleitung, Übersetzung, Kommentar, Giessen, 1915.

Ginza (übersetzt und erklärt), Göttingen, 1925.

Mandäische Liturgien (mitgeteilt, übersetzt, und erklärt), Berlin, 1920.

Macuch, R.

Handbook of Classical and Modern Mandaic, Berlin, 1965 (available only after the present MS had been completed).

Nöldeke, T.

Mandäische Grammatik, Halle, 1875.

Pallis, S. A.
Mandaean Studies, translated by E. H. Pallis, London, 1926.
Rosenthal, F.
Die aramäistische Forschung seit Th. Nöldeke's Veröffentlichungen, Leiden, 1939; on magic bowls, see pp. 218–23, 233–35.
Schwab, M.
"Vocabulaire de l'angélologie d'après les manuscrits hébreux de la Bibliothèque nationale," in *Mémoires présentés à l'Académie des inscriptions et belles-lettres*, 1st ser., vol. 10, Paris, 1897, pp. 113–430.
Thompson, R. C.
The Devils and Evil Spirits of Babylonia, vol. 1, London, 1903; vol. 2 London, 1904.

Magical Texts

For details of magic bowls published prior to 1913, see Montgomery (AIT, pp. 16–22). Rosenthal brings this survey down to 1939 (AF, pp. 34–35, 218–23, 233–5). Texts published since 1939 are among those noted below.

Albright, W. F.
"An Aramaic Magical Text in Hebrew from the Seventh Century B.C.," in *BASOR*, no. 76 (1939), pp. 5–11.
Driver, G. R.
"A Magic Bowl," in *RA*, vol. 27 (1930), pp. 61–64.
"An Aramaic Inscription in the Cuneiform Script," in *AfO*, vol. 3 (1926), pp. 47–53.
Drower, E. S.
"A Mandaean Phylactery," in *Iraq*, vol. 5 (1938), pp. 31–54.
"A Phylactery for Rue," in *Or*, vol. 15 (1946), pp. 324–46.
"Shafta d Pishra d Ainia," in *JRAS*, 1937, pp. 589–611; 1938, pp. 1–20.
"Three Mandaean Phylacteries," in *JRAS*, 1939, pp. 397–406.
Gordon, C. H.
"An Aramaic Exorcism," in *AO*, vol. 6 (1934), pp. 466–74.
"An Aramaic Incantation," in *AASOR*, vol. 14 (1934), pp. 141–3.
"An Incantation in Estrangelo Script," in *Or*, vol. 18 (1949), pp. 336–41.
"Aramaic and Mandaic Magical Bowls," in *AO*, vol. 9 (1937), pp. 84–106 (eight bowls).
"Aramaic Incantation Bowls," in *Or*, vol. 10 (1941), pp. 116–41 (nine bowls); pp. 272–84 (two bowls and notes on others); pp. 339–60 (notes on bowls in various museums).
"Aramaic Magical Bowls in the Istanbul and Baghdad Museums," in *AO*, vol. 6 (1934), pp. 319–34 (six bowls).
"The Aramaic Incantation in Cuneiform," in *AfO*, vol. 12 (1938), pp. 105–17.
"Two Magic Bowls in Teheran," in *Or*, vol. 20 (1951), pp. 306–15.
Layard, A. H.
Discoveries in the Ruins of Nineveh and Babylon, London, 1853. On pp. 521–2 a bowl appears whose inscription is described by S. A. Pallis as being Mandaean (*Mandaean Bibliography*, p. 153), but Layard's hand-drawn facsimile does not support this view.

Lidzbarski, M.
"Ein mandäisches Amulett," in *Florilegium dédiés à M. le Marquis Melchior de Vogüé*, Paris, 1909, pp. 349–73.
"Mandäische Zaubertexte," in *Ephemeris für Semitische Epigraphik*, vol. 1 (1962), pp. 89–106 (five bowls).

Montgomery, J. A.
"A Magical Bowl-Text and the Original Script of the Manichaeans," in *JAOS*, vol. 32 (1912), pp. 434–8.
Aramaic Incantation Texts from Nippur, Philadelphia, 1913 (forty bowls, with two other texts). For a long review of this, see GBA I and II.

Narqis, M.
"An Aramaic Incantation," in *Tarbiz*, vol. 6 (1934), pp. 106–7.

Obermann, J.
"Two Magic Bowls: New Incantation Texts from Mesopotamia," in *AJSL*, vol. 57 (1940), pp. 1–31.

Pognon, H.
Inscriptions mandaïtes des coupes de Khouabir, Paris, 1898 (thirty-one bowls).
"Une incantation contre les génies malfaisants en Mandaïte," in *Mémoires de la Société de linguistique de Paris*, vol. 8 (1894), pp. 193–234.

Rossell, W. H.
A Handbook of Aramaic Magical Texts, Ringwood Borough, N.J., 1953 (thirty texts, all previously published).

Spoer, H. H.
"Arabic Magic Medicinal Bowls," in *JAOS*, vol. 55 (1935), pp. 237–56 (two bowls).

Teixidor, J.
"The Syriac Incantation Bowls in the Iraq Museum," in *Sumer*, vol. 18 (1962), pp. 51–62.

Yamauchi, E. M.
"Aramaic Magic Bowls," in *JAOS*, vol. 85 (1965), pp. 511–23 (one Aramaic bowl from Nehavand, Iran).
Mandaean Incantation Texts (1964 dissertation), Ann Arbor, Mich., 1966 (fifty-two texts, all previously published by Pognon, Lidzbarski, Montgomery, Driver, and Gordon).

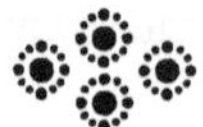

GLOSSARIES

All references are to the line in the designated text; prepositions, etc., are not cited exhaustively. A page number refers to a note on the word in question.

1. Proper Names in Texts A and B (Jewish Aramaic)

Babai: A 2, 3, 4, p. 4
Dilriʿiel: A 1, p. 4
El: A 4, p. 5
El-El: A 1, p. 4
Jannai: B 2, p. 8; B 5, 6, 8
Jerusalemite: A 3, p. 5
Maḥlapta: A 2, p. 4; A 3, 4
Mruduk: A 3, p. 5
Qristia: A 3, p. 5
Razhel: B 3, p. 8
Sariel: A 1, p. 4
Shaddai: A 4, p. 5; B 9, p. 10
Shlishiel: A 1, p. 4
YY: B 3, p. 8
Zgus: B 4, p. 9
Zkut: B 2, 3, p. 8; B 4; cf. ZHWT, B 3; ZKWŠ, B 6

2. Texts A and B (excluding names)

ʾWBʾ; pl. ʾWBYN: A 2, p. 4
ʾZL: A 1, p. 4
ʾYYN: B 7, p. 9
ʾLN: B 8, p. 9
ʾSWTʾ: B 3
ʾSR: B 1, p. 8
ʾTWN: A 1

B: A 2
BYŠ: B 3, 4
BYTʾ: A 2; B 3
BSR: B 4
BR: A 2; B 1
BRʾ: B 6
BT: A 3

GDʾ; pl. GDYʾ: B 9

D̲: A 2; B 4
DY: A 2
DYWʾ; pl. cst. DYWYY: B 6, p. 9; pl., B 8
DYRʾ: B 3, p. 8

HWS: B 6, 7
HṬR: B 1, p. 8
HYLʾ; pl. cst. HYYLY: B 3
HYTMʾ: B 9, p. 10
HLZ: A 1, p. 4
HMD: B 5
HMŠH: A 1, p. 4
HTM: A 4, p. 5; B 1, p. 8; B 4

YT: A 2

KBŠ: A 2
KWL: B 9
KTB: B 5
KTT: B 4

LHŠ: B 7

MHY: B 8
ML'K', pl.: A 1, p. 4
MRR, Aph.: A 2, p. 4

NTQ: B 7, p. 9

S'NSWT: B 8, p. 9
SYM'N': B 8, p. 10; B 9
SNY; p.part. pl. SNYY': B 8, p. 9

ʿDR I: B 4, p. 8

ʿZQT': A 4, p. 5
ʿL: A 2

PGR: B 2
PṢY, Aph.: B 3, p. 8

ṢWR, p.part.: A 4, p. 5

QZZ, Pa.: B 5, p. 9

RBT: A 3, p. 5
RHB, Aph.: B 6, p. 9
RWH: B 2, p. 8
RHY': A 2
RYGYL: A 3, p. 5

ŠWY, Pa.: B 8

THT: A 3

3. Proper Names in Texts C, D, and E (Mandaic)

Names which do not occur in MD are asterisked.

*Adrban: D 12, 12, pp. 39–40
*Akmahin: D 16, p. 45
*Antun (?): D 13, 13, p. 41
Anush: E 3, p. 51
*Anushtai: E 4, p. 52
*Aruhun: D 12, p. 40
Asrel: E 17, p. 57
*Azel: E 17, p. 57

Bhaq: C 20, p. 26
Bhar: E 4, p. 52
*Buktuya (BUKTY'): D 3, p. 33; BUKTWY': D 9, 10, 11, 11, 14, 14, 17, 18
*Busai: E 3, p. 51; E 13, 13, 14, 14, 18
*Bzurgantai (BZWRG'NT'Y): C 3, pp. 16–17; C 9; BZRGWNT'Y: C 16; BZWRGWNT'Y: C 17, 19; BZWRGWN'T'Y: C 22

*Cain: D 16, p. 46

Dukt: E 3, p. 52; E 18
*Duktan (DWKTN): C 2, p. 16; DWKT'N: C 12, 16, 17, 19, 21, 23, 24; D̲WKT'N': C 9

*El ('YL): D 5, p. 34; cf. ʿYL, MD, p. 348

Gabriel: D 9, p. 38

*Hadriel: D 12, p. 40
*Halahkin: D 7, p. 36
*Hasdiel: D 12, p. 40
Hathmel(?): E 8, p. 53
*Hiel (Hailel?): D 12, p. 40
*Hldh (?): D 6, p. 35
*Hnaqel: E 17, p. 57
Hurmiṣ: C 6, p. 19

*Kabshiel: E 17, p. 57
Kbar-Ziwa: E 14, p. 56
*Krakel: E 17, p. 57
*Kushai: D 3, pp. 33–34; D 9, 10, 11, 11, 13, 14, 14, 17, 18
*Kʿwya: E 3, p. 52

Life: C 1, p. 16; C 16; E 1, 18
Lord of Greatness: E 8, p. 53

*Metatron: D 6, p. 35
*Michael: D 10, p. 38
*Moses (MŠH): D 12, 12, p. 40

*Nadriel: D 10, p. 38
*Narsai Dukt: E 3, p. 52; E 14, 18
Nurel: C 14, p. 22

*Prel: E 17, p. 57

4. Texts C, D, and E (excluding names)

Words or forms of words not recorded in MD are asterisked, as are words whose meanings in these texts are not in MD.

BMʾ D̲: E 12
BNʾTʾ (pl. of BRʾTʾ): C 16
BR: C 14; D 3; E 3, 9; pl. C 16; D 11, 15, 18, 18; E 4, 9, 14
BR HYYʾ: C 14–15, p. 23
BRʾ: E 8; Aph., E 5, p. 52
BRʾYʾ, pl.: C 26
BRGWDʾ: D 6, p. 35
BRYTʾ, pl.: D 4
BRK, Aph.: E 11
*BT: C 19; D 4, 9, 11, 11, 14, 14, 14, 17, 18; pl. D 11, 15, 18

*GʾS (imv. of KSS?): D 13, pp. 40–41
GBYNʾ: C 19
GBRʾ: C 19, p. 26
GDWLʾ, pl.: E 15, p. 56
GDPʾ, pl.: C 9, p. 20
GYRMʾ, pl.: C 4, pp. 17–18
GNPʾ, pl.: E 17
*GRBʾNʾ: D 16, p. 46

D̲: C 1; D 1; E 1; cf. D as the relative in WDZʾDWYʾ, D 11, p. 39
Dʾ: C 22, p. 27
DʾYWʾ: C 7; pl. C 8; D 7, p. 36; E 13, 14, 15
DHL: E 14
DWKTʾ: E 11
DWRʾ: C 7; D 2, 18; E 2, 17
DYWYʾ ṬʾBYʾ: D 8, p. 36
*DYWYʾ ṄWQʾBʾTʾ: C 16, p. 24
DYKR, pl.: D 14, 15, 16
DYQTʾ (?): D 7, p. 19
DKR, Aph. (?): D 16, p. 45
*DMʾ: C 15, p. 23
DMW DMW: E 16, p. 56
DMWTʾ, pl.: C 17, p. 25
DQQ: C 20

H (interrogative?): D 17
Hʾ: E 8, p. 53
HʾDYN: D 13
HʾHW: D 11
HʾZYN: C 6
HʾYLʾ: C 7; D 12; pl. E 12
HʾLYN: D 13
HʾMŠʾ: C 6, p. 19
HʾNʾ: E 10
HʾSYRTʾ: E 9, p. 54
HʾTMʾ: E 15
HBʾ: E 12
HBʾLʾ: E 11
HBRʾ, pl.: D 17
HGʾ(?): C 17, p. 25
*HDRʾ: D 12; pl. E 10, p. 54
HW: C 26; D 6
HWʾ ("to be"): C 15; D 2; E 2; etc.
HWʾ, Pa. ("to show"): E 11
*HWZʾYYʾ, pl.: D 8, p. 37
*HWṬ, Pa.: E 13, p. 56; E 14
HWMRYʾ (pl. of HWMʾRTʾ): E 13, 16
*HWS (HWŠ ?): D 13, pp. 40–41
*HWQ: C 20; Etta. C 22
*HWRʾYYʾ: D 8, p. 37
HZʾ: C 20; E 8, 8, 9
*HZʾ WMHZʾ: D 5, p. 34
HZʾNWN: E 9, p. 53
HZYN: C 12
HṬʾ: C 21
HYYʾ: C 1, p. 16; C 15, 16, p. 24; C 22, 25; E 1, 18
HYKLʾ: D 3, 18; E 2, 17
HYLMʾ, pl.: C 16
HYMYʾN: E 10, p. 54
HYNWN: E 13
HYRBʾ: E 16
*HYŠWKʾ: C 17, p. 25
HLʾ, Pa.: D 7, p. 36
HLYṢʾ: C 20; pl. C 20
HMRʾ: D 7
HSDʾ: D 12
HRBʾ, pl.: C 4, p. 18
HŠK: C 18, p. 25; Pa. E 13
HTM: C 9 (super.); D 16
HTMTʾ: C 15; D 17; E 1; HTʾMTʾ: D 1

W: C 7; etc.

ZʾWʾ: C 16, p. 24, D 4, 14
ZWD: E 5, p. 52
ZWH: C 20; ʿTZYHʾT: Etta. (?) C 21, 21
ZYWʾ: C 14, p. 23; D 12
ZYKR, pl.: C 16; D 8; cf. ZYKYʾ, D 18, p. 47
ZYMTʾ: C 10
ZYNʾ: D 7, p. 36
ZYQʾ: C 5, p. 18
ZKʾ (a. part. pl. ZʾKYN): C 16, p. 24; C 25; E 18
ZMʾ: D 11, p. 39
ZRʾ: E 9, p. 54

ʿSR: C 3; E 12; etc.
ʿŠYWL: C 3, p. 17

PGRʾ: C 17
PWG (?): C 5, p. 18
PYGʾ, pl.: D 8, p. 36
PYQDʾ, pl.: E 15
PKR: C 5, E 11
PS (imv. of PSS?): D 13, p. 41
*PSD, Aph.: E 12, p. 55
PRYKYʾ, pl.: E 12
PRSʾYYʾ, pl.: D 8, p. 37
PT: C 2, 9, 12, 16, 17, 21; E 4
PTYKRʾ, pl.: E 16

*Ṣʾ WTʾ: D 17, p. 46
*ṢWHTʾ: D 7, p. 36
ṢMR II, Etta.: E 14

QʾLʾ: D 7
QDWM: E 7, p. 53
*QDYM: D 6, p. 35
QWM: E 8
QYNYʾNʾ: D 11; E 5
QYRYʾ: C 18
*QMʿ: C 14, p. 23
QRʾ: E 9; Ethpe. E 6
*QRYWʾ, pl.: E 7, 7, p. 53

RʾBWTʾ: E 8, p. 53
RʾZʾ: C 3, p. 17; C 20; E 9; pl. C 16; E 5, 11
RBʾ: C 14; D 7, 13; E 6, 10; f. RBTYʾ: D 2
*RBWTʾ (pl. of RWBʾN?): D 12, p. 40; cf. RʾBWTʾ, E 8, p. 53
*RGZʾ: C 18, p. 25
RGL: E 11
RHM (a. part. RHYM, RʾHYM): D 6, 6
RHMʾ, pl.: E 14
*RWBGʾN: C 19, p. 26
RWGZʾ: C 20; E 16
RWHʾ, pl.: D 15; E 16
RYŠʾ: C 10; E 10; pl. E 17
RQYHʾ C 8, p. 20; D 13 (?), p. 41
*RTT, Aph.: D 9, p. 38

ŠʾLYṬʾ, pl.: E 16
ŠʾQʾ, pl.: E 17
ŠBʾ, III Aph.: D 4, p. 34; D 16
*ŠBT: D 9, p. 38
*ŠDQ, Pa.: E 17, pp. 56–57
ŠWBʾ: D 13, p. 41
*ŠWBʿʾ: E 9, p. 54; E 16
ŠWMʾ: C 1; D 5; E 1, 17; pl. C 8, D 17
ŠWMYʾ: E 6, 6, 7, 9
ŠYDʾ, pl.: D 8; E 13, 15
*ŠYRŠWRʾ: C 13, p. 22
ŠLṬ, Pa.: E 16
ŠLM: D 18, p. 47
ŠMʾ: C 11, p. 22
ŠMŠ, Pa.: D 6
ŠRʾ, Etta.: D 16; E 15, 15
ŠRʾGʾ, pl.: E 13
ŠRʾRʾ: C 15, pp. 23–24; C 23; D 2
ŠTʾ: D 7

TBR: E 17, 17; Ethpe. E 15
TWTYʾ: C 6
TYTʾYʾ, pl.: C 7, p. 19
TʿM (for ṬʿM ?): D 16, p. 45
TQYP: D 12
TRYSʾR: E 9, p. 54; E 16

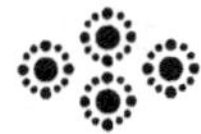

GENERAL INDEX

www.ingramcontent.com/pod-product-compliance
Lightning Source LLC
LaVergne TN
LVHW082158080826
844660LV00046B/1268

9781487579180